Your Presence Is Enough

To order additional copies, please contact us.
BookSurge, LLC
www.booksurge.com
1-866-308-6235
orders@booksurge.com

JULIA
TINDALL

YOUR PRESENCE IS
ENOUGH

2006

Your Presence Is Enough

CONTENTS

ACKNOWLEDGEMENTS

This book could not have been written without the help of my spiritual warrior friends; my jnana yoga group that meets every Tuesday to process and clear egoic conditioning. Many of the meditations and exercises outlined in the book were developed during our Tuesday groups and some of the examples described are from the life-experience of my Sacramento jnana yoga students.

For help in editing I wish to thank Chris Mitchell for his clarity and encouragement; Whitney Campbell for his enthusiasm; Aimee Campbell for her diligence; Theodora Wilner for her assistance; Vicki Andreotti for her insight into the victim; Gail Fahey for her great ideas on shadow; Luis Diaz for his work on clearing patterns; and Kathi Neff for all her love, support and ideas. For the imagery of the tug-of-war I acknowledge the infamous Viktor. For her help with formatting at midnight in Waikiki, I thank Vicki Hendersen. For cover photos, I honor Bruce Robinson and Jane Derry.

For starting me on the path of jnana yoga, I acknowledge yogi Baba. For encouraging me to clear my shadow and commit fully to the path of awakening, I thank Leslie Temple-Thurston.

INTRODUCTION

Presence is the greatest gift we can give ourselves and others. Presence means that our awareness is focused on the current moment, with no concern for the future or past. Mind chatter is at a minimum, leaving us alert, sensitive and responsive. We all want to feel the strength, openness and love that Presence brings, but how can we be there all the time?

This book offers the keys to living a joy-filled life by systematically dissolving the issues that block our Presence. We analyze step-by-step some of the major ways that we get caught up in our emotions, dramas and stories and through self-inquiry we gradually learn to let them go.

The spiritual path of self-inquiry (jnana yoga) is the hero's journey towards Presence, wholeness and freedom. *Wholeness* comes from reclaiming all of our parts, both our humanness and our Divinity. We explore our shadow side, the aspects of ourselves that we reject or hide in our unconscious. We discover our authentic Selves as we learn to let go of the mask we present to the world. We expand our light side, the positive traits of the higher self, waking up to the reality of our Divinity.

Freedom comes from letting go of the veils of beliefs and conditioned patterns that cover up our authentic Selves. As children we learn to see the world through a filter of these veils. It's like peering out through blinders. We don't see the big picture. Self-inquiry helps to uncover these veils, and more and more light enters our being. The filter changes. We see more of the picture. We feel better, more expanded. We have more energy, more clarity, and our *Presence* naturally deepens.

The exercises presented in this book help us to clear these veils from our ego/mind so that by the time we get to Chapter 20 and ask, "Who am I?" we are prepared and ready to shed our layers of illusion, step out of the box of our neurosis and drop into awareness of our true Selves. In this state we can relax deeply into the Presence that we are. Love and joy flow effortlessly from our very being. We embrace each moment as perfect and know that indeed our *Presence is Enough.*

How to use this book....

You may wish to start or join a group to encourage each other to explore the material presented here. In a group we can reflect each others' behaviors and patterns and trigger new awareness by listening to each other. This greatly speeds up our ability to see our self-made illusions. Having a regular group meeting encourages us to stay on track with our inquiry. We have people with whom we can share our insights, challenges and fears. This sharing helps us develop a close-knit web of friendships, a spiritual community that gives support, love and guidance for life; a precious gift indeed. All of the exercises in this book have been tried and tested on my Sacramento jnana group over many years and much of the input comes from these courageous students who have been willing to look deeply at themselves.

As an individual, I suggest reading the book through first, then going back and taking each chapter slowly, practicing a new exercise each day or each week. Then keep the book handy as a reference guide for times when certain issues arise in your everyday life. For example, if you find yourself dealing with anger, grief or shame, consult the appropriate chapters for reminders on ways to examine these feelings. Use the tools offered to help stay centered and present, despite the outer turbulence you may be experiencing.

This book is a continuation of my first book on jnana yoga, *"20 Questions for Enlightened Living"* and presents a program of deeper self-inquiry. We strengthen our ability to witness the workings of the ego and use clearing techniques to balance our polarized parts into one harmonious whole.

We live in accelerated times. It is becoming more and more important that we learn to clear our old programming so we can be as free and light as possible, functioning fully as the Divine Creators that we are. May your journey of discovery that *'Your Presence is Enough'* be filled with joy, love, light and delight!

If you are new to the spiritual path, please familiarize yourself with the terminology in the glossary.

Please note: In the text I refer to the Divine, God or Spirit. Feel free to substitute whichever term you use for the Creator.

THE WITNESS

The witness is the part of us that watches. It is neutral, dispassionate and non-judgmental. The witness observes what is passing before it and simply notices *what is so*. It doesn't analyze, worry or lament, nor does it have an opinion about anything. These are functions of the mind.

The witness watches our minds busily chattering away and observes our personalities moving us through our world as though it were all occurring on a television screen. It is one step removed from the drama of identification with thoughts and behaviors. As such the witness is a valuable ally for us to align with, especially if we are interested in waking up to the Truth of who we are.

To locate the witness...
Take a moment to become aware of the sounds around you. Notice any body sensations, the temperature of the room, the quality of the light. Notice your breath entering and leaving the body. As your awareness expands to encompass all this, notice that thought slows down or stops. Linger here a while. It is your witness that is aware.

As thoughts pop back into the mind, notice them, but then drop back again into the witnessing position by returning to awareness of the breath. Practice this a few times until you experience clearly that the witness can observe the mind, yet exists separately from it.

What's so....
What's so refers to whatever is going on in the moment, exactly as it is; reality in present time, without the mind's interpretations. We will refer to *what's so* frequently throughout the text.

RECLAIMING OUR POWER

Most of us are not living at our maximum potential. We hide our true nature behind approval-seeking behavior. We play it safe by staying in our comfort zone, instead of valuing ourselves enough to speak out for what we truly desire.

The next four chapters offer tools for reclaiming our latent power. We discover how to feel worthy by relaxing into acceptance of the way we are and finding strength in our Presence. We regain expression of our authentic Selves, let go of our limiting beliefs and regain physical and energetic balance. Now we are ready to expand and become all that we can be.

1.
HOW CAN I FEEL MY FULL WORTH?

"Lack of self-esteem is more arrogant than it is humble, suggesting the idea that God somehow created junk." Marianne Williamson, "Enchanted Love".

I was fourteen years old and excitedly preparing for my first school dance. I thought I looked great in my new purple suede boots and matching purple skirt. When I arrived, I felt an immediate attraction to a handsome boy. I hovered nearby, hoping he would notice me and ask me to dance. Instead of me, he danced with my best friend, ignoring me completely. I felt crushed, not pretty enough, not alluring enough, and sobbed all the way home. This was my introduction to the world of worthlessness.

The belief that we are not 'enough' is a learned belief that we take on as children. Events from our younger years reinforce this feeling of worthlessness and leave us with the sense of having gaping holes in our being. School teachers tell us we can't get it right. Parents yell at us for being naughty. We feel devastated, empty inside, so we attempt to fill the holes with external factors, like seeking worldly success or approval—a strategy that is doomed for failure.

When we feel 'enough', we are strong, powerful and secure. We are comfortable in any situation. We experience less stress and more ease. In this chapter we explore tools and techniques for dropping the attitude of worthlessness and begin to fill in our holes with self-esteem and acceptance. Our lives improve dramatically when we reconnect with our intrinsic self-worth.

The cost of feeling unworthy...

When we don't feel 'enough' and can't accept ourselves for the unique individuals that we are, we start compensating. We put on masks of make-up, fancy clothes, behaviors that we think will impress. We are not authentic, because we believe that if another person saw us for who we really are, they would not like us. We become workaholics, driven by the idea that we would feel 'enough' if we had lots of money or high position. Or we hide, either withdrawing from society or showing a brave face to the world despite our inner turmoil.

Most of our unhealthy behaviors and insecurities stem from this feeling of unworthiness. We feel unlovable and incompetent, which gives rise to our addictions, codependence, self-criticism, shame and self-sabotage. It's very hard to have a healthy relationship with these internal tapes running. How can we show up fully for another person and have something to offer if we think we are worthless? If we believe we have no light, we cannot shine.

The saboteur...

When we feel unworthy, part of our psyche turns against us and we create an inner saboteur. The saboteur acts out unconscious patterns of a belief which says, "I don't deserve success." It leads us to behave in ways that confirm the belief in our unworthiness, by keeping us locked into dysfunctional patterns and habits. For example, we may squander our money and find ourselves always broke; or we may spend too much time attending to trivialities and run late for important appointments. The good news is, that because the saboteur is our own creation, we can transform it as we awaken and mature, leading to new behaviors with different outcomes.

We begin the transformation process by first acknowledging the presence of our saboteur and thanking it for doing its job of illuminating our inner turmoil. Then we rewrite our agreement with the saboteur, making it into our ally. We give it a new task, which results in new, healthier behaviors.

Take a few quiet moments and have a conversation with the saboteur; it could look something like this:

(Note: It is helpful if someone can read this to you, or use the "Healing Meditations" CD.)

Close your eyes. Take a deep breath in and out. Relax.
Invite the inner saboteur to appear in front of you. Look at it with your mind's eye. Notice its shape, form and texture.
Ask it its name.
Ask the saboteur its job and its intention. Listen to the response.
Ask what it believes will happen when it does its job.
Go back to your childhood and see how the saboteur manifested for you then.
Notice if this same pattern has played out in later life.

Take a moment to reflect on how well the saboteur has done its job for you in the past. Thank it for that.

Now assign it another job. Rewrite your agreement with it in a new and more empowering way. *(For example, if the saboteur is highly critical, transform it into a cheerleader.)*

Thank it for cooperating.

Open your eyes and come back into the room.

When we did this exercise with my jnana yoga group, David got in touch with his saboteur and realized that its job was to prove he was loved by creating obstacles which people would first have to overcome. He remembered jeopardizing his birthday parties as a small child by telling his parents not to bother to make a party for him. He told them not to come to see him play Little League. Secretly he wanted his parents to overcome these objections. Then he would know they really loved him. When they took him at his word, he felt hurt and sad. David noticed that this sabotage pattern was still alive in his present day relationships, yet a little more hidden. He still created obstacles for his lovers and got upset when they didn't get over them. Now that he is aware of this pattern, he has rewritten his relationship with his saboteur so it can be his inner advocate and speak up for what he really wants in a clean, clear manner.

Self-rejection…

Most of us have a well-worn groove of self-judgment spinning around endlessly in our heads. We reject those parts of ourselves that don't match our picture of perfection and have shame around our body and its flaws. This creates a dark place of suffering for us that we feed with our mental attention.

It's a useful exercise to make a list of what we don't like about our personality and our physical traits. We put down on paper all the critical thoughts we secretly harbor about ourselves. The object here is not to indulge or validate our beliefs about our flaws, but simply to bring what is hidden within us into the light of our awareness. Once our self-rejection is out on the table for all to see, it no longer wields as much power over our psyche. This alone can create healing.

The next step is to look at our list and accept our self-rejection! We own and admit that we have opinions about ourselves, but the trick is, we don't judge the fact that we have opinions, we just observe them. We all have some degree of self-judgment. Yet by accepting that it is there, we can send compassion to our sweet self instead of more self-hatred, expanding the energy of love around the band of self-rejection. Then, if self-critical thoughts should pop back into the mind in future, we just observe they are there and let them fade into the background. As they are now a known factor, we can drop them more easily.

Here's an example of my inner dialogue:

I dislike the lines under my eyes. In my opinion they make me look old and ugly. Sometimes I cover them up with make-up. If I drop into the witnessing position and observe myself from a detached, neutral point of view, I notice that my personal 'I' is hating the lines. I accept that. Then I ask myself what it would feel like to love these lines just the way they are. I notice my resistance to loving them. My witness meets with that resistance without judgment. Then my feeling about these lines moves to a more neutral space, not rejecting nor adoring, just accepting.

My friend Judy brought up a great technique for transforming negative self-rejection thoughts. When she notices she is having one she identifies it as a 'trash thought' and sends it to her 'internal recycle bin' where she visualizes the thought being blown up! She does not judge herself for having these thoughts, she just transforms them and immediately sends her mental energy elsewhere.

When we discussed self-rejection in our jnana group, many issues around aging surfaced. Our internal pictures of perfection did not match our fat tummies, wrinkly faces and physical infirmities! Yet with changing physicality comes an opportunity to dwell more constantly in our radiant core. We can put more emphasis on internal beauty rather than external. The activities of younger people often lose their appeal. We start to live our lives differently and expand in new ways rather than being attached to past ways of living. I spend far more time on yoga and meditation practice now, rather then going shopping or to dance clubs and bars. The rewards are far more satisfying.

The myth of self-improvement...

The big trap of many religious, spiritual and psychological practices is that they instill in us the idea that we are not good enough as we are and we need to earn our way to heaven. Clinging to this idea can prevent us from truly accepting and loving ourselves. As children we were programmed to 'do' in order to receive praise and acceptance. Yet there's nothing we need to do in order to be lovable. Babies don't do anything and we still love them. We must let go of the need to perform and achieve, in order to feel worthy and instead practice acknowledging that our Presence is enough.

It's not that we get lazy and give up our healthy practices. It helps us feel better to exercise, meditate and still the mind. Yet achieving perfection in a practice is not necessary in order for us to feel 'enough' right now! Can we let go of our attachment to being different from the way we are and focus on our fullness rather than our imperfections? We are all unique expressions of God regardless of how we manifest ourselves. The world would not be the same without us. We all have our own unique gifts to offer and challenges to face.

Who's comparing?

The ego loves comparison! It wants to feel superior, as this makes us feel strong and establishes us on the pecking order of life. The trouble is that comparison immediately destroys our ability to appreciate our unique place in the world. It highlights areas where we are inferior to others and at some point our inner critic is activated. We stop loving ourselves just as we are. Envy arises, and with it the desire to be different.

When we give up the notion that we are inferior or superior in any way and we simply express or observe who we are, we move out of the duality of comparison and into a loving unity with all things. Instead of feeling diminished by someone else's good qualities, we can use them as an inspiration for creating new possibilities for ourselves to expand in new ways. I have a yogini friend who dresses and looks like a glamorous goddess! I used to feel some envy being around her, but now I use her loveliness to inspire me to greater heights of dress awareness so I can honor my own femininity!

Approval-seeking…

We want approval because at our core we feel insecure, separate and unloved. A hit of approval temporarily bolsters our confidence and hides these deeper feelings of unworthiness. Hence our egos are very preoccupied with what people think of us. Gaining approval becomes such an insidious addiction that we'll do almost anything to get it. We take on too much responsibility, say 'yes' when we mean 'no', let others control us and become codependent people-pleasers. We give precious power and energy to this imaginary God of approval, setting up a vicious cycle of needing ever more approval in order to feel worthy again.

What if the world's supply of approval ran out? We would stop acting to please others and instead act with authenticity! We can start that now. We can use our witness to examine the motivations for our actions. If we are offering a service to someone with no attachment to the outcome, we are acting out our truth. My friend Sam likes to call this 'angeling'. If we want approval for our action we have attachment, which taints the act with a different energy. Asking the question, "Am I doing this to gain approval or is this what I really want to do?" helps us become more conscious of our motivations.

Turning it around…

Here are some other useful tools for helping us feel our innate worthiness.

- We can enjoy a 'feeling enough' break during the day by taking a couple of deep breaths and dropping into our own beloved Presence, feeling the gift of our magnificent selves, just as we are.
- When we take things personally it's easy to feel worthless. We must differentiate between what is true and what is a projection from someone else.
- Give love, *be* love, by practicing karma yoga, the yoga of selfless service to others; it catapults us out of our obsession with ourselves and our shortcomings.
- Being in integrity: that is, speaking our truth, being our word.
- Doing the best we can in all situations. Striving for excellence (our own personal best) rather than perfection (an impossible goal).
- We stop judging ourselves. We feel deeply that being without achieving is OK and our simple Presence is a blessing to the planet.
- External actions reflect how we feel about ourselves, so if we want to shift our relationship with worthlessness we can start with external factors and notice that over time our internal attitude will change too. If we value ourselves enough, we feed ourselves nutritious, healthy food. We allow ourselves playtime and exercise. We keep the body clean. We live in a harmonious environment.
- If we practice seeing worthiness in everyone else, everywhere, our whole world will change! We can choose to see the cup half full rather than half empty. How many times in a day do we tell someone that they are 'not enough' by making them wrong or disapproving of them? We can consciously shift that into validating them instead. When we affirm that they are worthy, we affirm it for ourselves too.

Ultimately…

In Truth we are not flawed at all. We are Divine beings, perfectly expressed in human form. Once we start to sink into a state of deep Presence and stop identifying with all our stories about ourselves, we know beyond a doubt that this Presence is enough. A situation may arise where, in the past, our tape of unworthiness would have played loud and clear. Now it may still play softly in the background, but we no longer feed it energy and attention. We feel full and complete and see clearly that any ideas to the contrary just overlay the Truth of who we are. This is freedom! We emanate a love that touches everyone and our Presence becomes a blessing.

"How can God be God if I am less worthy than you?"—Kathy Neff

When we feel we're 'enough'...

We know we're 'enough' when:

- Someone puts us down and we see their pain and don't take it personally.
- We laugh at ourselves when we fail.
- We no longer need approval, which gives rise to real personal power.
- We let go of wanting to be different from the way we already are.
- It's no longer OK for us to be abused.
- Self-criticism stops and we accept ourselves fully, warts and all.
- We feel into our fullness rather than focusing on the parts of ourselves that we reject.
- People are drawn to us—our Presence becomes attractive and grounding to others.
- Miracles occur—we manifest more easily.
- We step out of the box of duality that gives rise to comparisons.
- We are authentic and speak our truth.
- We stop taking life so seriously—outcomes and attachments are less important.
- We feel the flow of life in its perfection.
- Fear dissolves...
- We are open, available and loving. There is more joy and fullness in each moment.
- We stop wanting—desires tend to fall away.

Examples:

Victoria came to Harbin Hot Springs on a weekend retreat with me. She spent the day relaxing in the mineral baths and was feeling great. Then she came up to the house where our group was staying and saw two incredibly glamorous women already there. She compared her physical appearance to theirs and felt herself to be somehow lacking. Feeling terrible, she walked outside and met my friend Rocky. She told him what she was feeling. He reminded her to 'be who you are', that we are not our external package! He also cautioned her about making assumptions about others. We don't know their internal landscape! With those reminders, Victoria managed to let go of her self- judgment and came back to enjoy a wonderful weekend.

John says his parents have a whole list of reasons as to why he is 'not enough'—and the list doesn't change! But he can change. He does not choose to buy into their list and feel unworthy when he is around them. Instead he focuses on feeling love for them and himself.

When I sit with my enlightened teachers and marvel at their ability to read people and help them clear ego, my own sense of unworthiness as a teacher can get triggered. One time I was with Paul Lowe and complained to him about my shortcomings. His response was very clear and direct: "Get over yourself! We all have unique gifts and ways to communicate and we all do it at the level we can. There will always be someone more or less awake than you. So be the teacher to those who are less awake and don't worry about the rest!"

Pat is an action-oriented person and values herself by what she gets done in a day. So one day she took a day and did no tasks—to practice feeling worthy without having to achieve anything. She felt so relaxed and full after this that she now devotes one day a week to this practice!

Exercises:
1. Write down/discuss all the ways feeling unworthy manifests in your life and how it hinders you. How do you compensate for this?
2. Complete the line, "I would feel enough if. ..." Look at the list again, from the vantage point of the witness, detached from personality. If you had all these things on your list how would you feel? Can you allow yourself to feel that right now? Notice you can have the feeling even if you don't have those things. Can you give yourself permission to have that feeling more often? It's a choice.
3. Look at how you make negative comparisons between yourself and others. How can you turn them into inspiration?
4. In pairs: Which parts of yourself do you reject? Write a list. Do this with a friend. Give your lists to each other and read out your friend's list as though you were they. Your friend then transforms himself into your guardian angel and speaks to you about this list. Notice the compassion that arises and how you feel about that same list now. Get your own list back and read it again. See if the charge around those issues has lessened.

God gives us two great gifts:
1. Obstacles to overcome, e.g. a critical boss.
2. Tools to overcome the obstacles, e.g. a strong inner advocate.
When we think we are our obstacles, we say, "I'm not enough."
When we think we are our tools, the ego-self says, "I'm special."
Neither is true. Identifying with either of them limits our universe. We are far more than any obstacle or tool we can possibly imagine.

2.
HOW CAN WE BE AUTHENTIC?

Mid-life crisis occurs when the soul can't handle even one more inauthentic moment!

When I first met Paul Lowe, one of my teachers, he looked me right in the eye and said, "You're not honest!" At that time I had no idea what he meant. I considered myself an honest person who didn't tell lies. Yet with hindsight I know exactly what he saw. I wasn't being authentic! An expert weaver of the mask of many smiles, I was consistently nice to everyone whether I felt like it or not. I hid behind this people-pleasing, codependent behavior. The real Julia with all of her shadow and her power was pushed deep into the background. People only got a half of me, which didn't do me or them any favors.

Authenticity is acting in alignment with our spirit. It's about expressing and being who we truly are as souls without the restriction of being attached to a desired outcome. We speak from the heart and are congruent in behavior, feeling and speech. Every time we are authentic and we deliver the truth upon request, we create healing and our frequency level is raised (the rate at which our energy field vibrates). Those around us sense the truth of our words and trust is established. When we are not authentic, we create discord and dis-ease. There is a sense of mistrust and our frequency drops.

Why we shut down our expression...
Babies are authentic. They scream and let their feelings out until they are gone. This may be the one time in our lives that our authentic selves are truly honored. It's deemed acceptable for babies to cry when they're hungry or wet and make cooing baby noises when they're happy. Then as infants we make noises and act wild...until our parents tell us to be quiet and behave, that is, conform to the way *they* want us to be. That's when we start to shut down. It upsets us that we have somehow offended those we love, so we hide our authentic expression.

As we grow older we become reluctant to drag that hidden part of us back out because we remember that it hurts the ones we love and makes them angry. The memory of that pain stops us from behaving authentically. The hiding strategy that was helpful for us as children becomes unhealthy for us as adults. It blocks our expression of joy! Any time we are playing the game of concealing who we are there is less energy available for our creative juice, less true happiness and fulfillment.

How do we hide?
Here are some examples of my personal favorite ways to hide:
Being nice, (people-pleasing), censoring my speech because of fear of disapproval.
Codependent behavior—accepting abuse because I am too afraid of confrontation.
My own personal 'cloaking device'—silence, withdrawal, not communicating, isolation.
Making assumptions and not asking for clarity because I am afraid of the truth.
Worrying, not being in the moment.
Humor, playing the clown (when it's not authentic).
Being busy, shopping, alcohol, consumption eating.
Displaying anger rather than examining my wound behind the trigger.
Armoring—not risking being vulnerable, pretending.

It's useful to write a list of our own personal hiding strategies and then to be conscious as we do them. We can take steps to reverse these behaviors. As our courage increases, we come out of hiding more and more, bringing our authentic selves out to engage with the world.

The mask…
The mask is the outermost layer of our personality, the self-image that we present to the world. It is an idealized self-image, an attempt to portray the perfect picture of who we think we ought to be. We developed our mask as children to help us survive when times got tough. It was an attempt to become perfect in order to avoid further hurts. We believed we were not acceptable just as we were so the mask was formed in the hope that it would gain us love and acceptance. The only problem is that now we believe we *are* that mask. We think we have to defend it, further sustaining our feelings of inadequacy. In fact, people instinctively reject the mask and the insecurities it hides, but we often misinterpret this as a call for a more perfect mask, creating a vicious cycle of phoniness.

Any time we act differently from the way we truly feel in the moment, we are wearing the mask. If we can witness ourselves doing this, we can go deeper with our inquiry and ask what kind of impression we are trying to create with this mask and why. It's helpful to see the workings of our ego with as much clarity as possible. Then we can make different choices and start to act authentically, in alignment with our spirit's true desires.

We are only ready to drop the mask when we are willing to face our shadow selves and take full responsibility for all of our human traits. Then the defense of the mask is no longer needed. Dropping the mask brings us face to face with our true nature, with all its human strengths and weaknesses. We may even re-experience the childhood hurts that gave rise to the mask in the first place, but with the help of our witness, we can just be with those uncomfortable feelings without needing to hide them away. Now we have a chance of truly accepting ourselves as we are and giving ourselves the respect we deserve. This enables us to express ourselves authentically and feel the empowerment that timely expression brings.

The nature of truth…

There is a difference between egoic (relative) and universal truth. Universal Truth is an expression of soul consciousness and is changeless. It is eternal Truth manifesting in this world as Divine Presence. Relative truth expresses our partialities; for example, we prefer red not blue. This is the domain of the mind and personality. It is not cognizant of the whole so it cannot know absolute Truth. It is relative truth that we are concerned with when we talk about 'speaking our truth'.

Delivering truth…

Vern was proud of his commitment to honesty. He had lots of girlfriends and made sure they all knew about each other. Nothing was kept hidden. Vern was a passionate man and at any moment, he might turn to one of them and say, "I will love you till the day I die," or "You are so special. I will always want you in my life." The women believed him. The trouble was, Vern did not know where his true heart lay. This 'truth' that he spouted in the moment changed a day or two later. He left behind him a string of broken-hearted women. I know. I was one of them.

Our degree of authenticity is a function of how well we know ourselves.

We must learn to discern between mind chatter and real feelings. What is our gut feeling? Our guts don't lie! We can practice becoming aware of sensations in our physical bodies, feeling our emotions, our energy field, and disconnecting from what the mind thinks should be happening. If we make a commitment to truth, even though it is relative truth, our capacity for authenticity will strengthen and grow over time.

Being truly authentic requires us to speak up or act in the moment, letting go of our tendency to withhold, wiggle and edit. Can we be real, allowing the shape of the moment to guide us as to how and when to express ourselves? Sometimes speaking our truth can feel very scary and it takes a lot of courage to trust in the outcome. Yet the more we practice, the more we create a deeper connection with our true Self and a trust in our internal guidance.

If we wish to share a truth with a friend, the first step is to ask permission, to see if the person is receptive and if this is a good time. We make 'I' statements so it doesn't feel like an attack and we speak from the heart rather than from ego, so our friend can hear us and receive what we are saying.

For example, if we are feeling angry at someone, we can let out our anger by banging a pillow or yelling in the car before we speak to them about what is bothering us. Then when the anger energy is gone we can have a conversation that connects us rather than creates more separation. We might say, "I felt angry at you when you left me abruptly the other day, when I had carved out time to be with you. I felt disappointed as I enjoy being with you; so I ask that if, in the future, we have a date set up, that you honor our time agreements. Are you willing to do that?" Speaking in this way helps to ring the bell of truth in the hearts of our friends so any seemingly harsh words spoken over time can bear the sweetest fruit.

When we withhold our truth to take care of someone else's feelings so that they don't feel uncomfortable, we are supporting their neurosis. We are holding them in a space of 'not able to handle the truth'. Can we be fearless in our own expression and as clean with it as possible? Truth is often the simplest, most straightforward position and is best stated in a calm manner, without the emotional charge of judgment.

Asking for what we want…
Being authentic requires us to be lion-hearted and courageous. How often are we too afraid to ask for 100% of what we want? We are afraid of failure, getting hurt or losing face, so it's easier to stay in our own little box of safety, passing up opportunities and missing out on fun, joy and fulfillment. Of

course, we must be prepared to hear a 'no' and face possible rejection. Then we can negotiate. Without the courage to express our desires, we lead lukewarm lives. Is this really what we want? What if we could take a risk and tell that person across the crowded room we feel an attraction towards them and would like to get to know them better? How would they ever know if we don't say anything?

Asking for support to live out our dreams is a great practice for voicing our authentic desires. In our jnana group, miracles occurred when we did an exercise around this. *David wanted to make a CD of his flute playing. He had no clue as to how to start this process. But members of the group did. He was invited to visit the home of a record producer and learn the trade from there. He ended up making his CD and bringing his dream into fruition.*

Living the authentic life...

If we recall the definition of authenticity, which is to live in alignment with our spirit (soul), we can ask, "Are we congruent with our souls in our daily lives or are we selling our soul?" The fantasy of the American dream suckers us into pursuing the path of material success, whereby our souls are aligned with the goals of materialism. This is a goal-oriented treadmill that consistently draws our energy. There's a promise of satisfaction, but somehow it never delivers. We are left wanting more. The bigger house, faster car, fancier clothes. There's a sense of lack, of something missing.

To be congruent we must examine the split between our personality and our spirit, questioning the core beliefs of our lives to see if they are still true. We must be brave enough to see what chapters in our lives are ready to close and how we can spiral up to the next level, recognizing any fears and fallacies that have held us back. We examine congruence in regards to work, play, friendships, spiritual practice and how we treat the planet. We know when these aspects of our lives are in alignment with our spirit, because they bring us peace and joy and we feel satisfied at a deep level.

Where is it we need to be? Where do we belong? One student of mine, Sarah, was in a health club stretching before she began to exercise. She is a tall lady and a member of the staff told her not to stretch as she was taking up too much room! She came to my yoga class later that day and was invited to take up as much space as possible! Sarah felt at home with the yoga and decided the health club is not an environment where she can be her authentic self, so she no longer goes there.

Impeccability…

Impeccability refers to how we use our energy and is another aspect of authenticity. We are impeccable when we use our energy in a balanced way, in alignment with our spirit. We are responsible for our world, we own who we are without fear and we let go of approval-seeking behaviors. We have 100% integrity and say what we mean and mean what we say. This opens our heart and creates trust between us and other people. Others know that when we speak to them we are motivated by love and compassion, rather than any ego-based desires. It is the pre-requisite for being a teacher. We use truth to assist students rather than destroy them.

One activity that leads us away from impeccability is the tendency to gossip. Gossiping is when we talk about a person with judgment behind their back and is often laden with assumptions and speculations. Before we open our mouths to gossip we can always ask ourselves what the purpose and motivation is behind it. Is the intent constructive or destructive? Gossip takes its toll. First, it wastes precious energy that we could better spend processing ourselves. Secondly, the person we're taking about is being sent 'energetic poison arrows' that affect their energy. This creates a karmic backlash we would do well to avoid. If a friend tries to reel us into gossiping about someone, it's better not to participate. We can just say, "Bless them" and move on to talk about what is real and alive with those present.

Benefits of being authentic…

When we are authentic, we set ourselves free from society's conditioning and our own need to control and play safe. We overcome our fear of losing approval or hurting someone. We are at peace with ourselves. Being authentic helps us embrace our shadow side and witness it with compassion rather than hiding from it. Having dropped our mask of pretension and artificiality, we feel more alive, more creative and experience a greater sense of freedom and joy.

Authenticity fosters intimacy and trust and keeps our relationships alive and juicy. We are most lovable when we are at our most transparent and this openness touches everyone around us! People trust us to be real with them, to be honest and present. Our interactions are elevated and we discuss heartfelt, poignant questions rather than indulging in idle chitchat. We become natural and loose, flowering into our true nature.

We all have an individual flow, our personal current in the river of life. It's an expression of who we are that is unique to us and shines forth when we let go of our mask and stop trying to conform. It's deep down, not at the surface and is relaxed, smooth and real. Living happily and fearlessly in this way brings us to our maximum potential. When we can be with whatever we feel without looking for approval or conformity and without questioning if it's safe or silly, we come alive, we are spontaneous. This present moment is our priority and life becomes more fulfilling.

Examples:

When I was young I adopted the mask of being the good little girl to win my family's love. I never made waves or upset anyone, even at the cost of my own pain. With romantic partners I have had a tendency to be codependent for the same reason. To gain and retain their love, I would set my needs aside rather than trusting I would be loved for my real Self. As I progressed with my spiritual journey, I realized this mask limited my self-expression, stifled my assertiveness and squelched my joy. Yet this behavior is so ingrained, I have to constantly stay vigilant in order to not slip back into the familiar patterns of my youth.

My friend Marie's brother is a dentist. She has always gone to him for dental care yet has had the feeling that he doesn't really want to treat her. She even felt like he was not giving her the best dental treatment. So eventually she went to another dentist, who confirmed that her teeth were in bad shape. She had to tell her brother she no longer wanted him as her dentist and she felt really hurt that he had not taken good care of her. This was tough for her to do, but she honored herself by speaking up and making the change.

Joan's parents were divorced and did not get along. Joan was getting married and was afraid to invite them both to the wedding. But the truth was, she really wanted them both there. So she asked each of them to come and to behave peacefully. They honored her request and in asking for what she wanted, Joan created a magical wedding day for herself!

Exercises:
1. List all the ways you hide. Pick one and reverse the behavior this week.
2. Make a list of the ways you are not being congruent in daily life. Pick one and change it.
3. Talk to yourself in the mirror. Say inauthentic things and then truthful things. Notice how your looks change! We are so much more beautiful when we are authentic. We are luminous, shining clearly, even through tears.
4. Make it a practice this week to ask for what you want.
5. Notice how you feel when you are gossiping. Start to cut it out.

6. Start to share what you would normally withhold; that is, speak your truth from that authentic place of the heart.

7. Discuss with a partner: "What do you really want that you have never asked for?"

8. When did you last act or speak inauthentically? Why did you withhold? What happened as a result?

The Egyptian mystery school had a new initiate. She was smart and intuitive and did well in her studies. In her last test before graduation, she was taken to a labyrinth. As she walked around through the labyrinth, she was tested with beautiful men, riches and pleasures of the senses. She ignored them all. Then came the last test. She had to choose a door to exit. One door led to death and the other to enlightenment. She chose the left door and was about to step through it when suddenly her master appeared. She said, "My dear, you've done very well, but this is the wrong door. You need to choose the other one." She faltered, doubting her instincts. She walked through the door on the right and died.

3.
HOW DO I LIMIT MY POWER?

The main limitations we have in life are the ones we give ourselves. We all want peace and fulfillment and can *be* in that state, whatever our physical attributes, life situation or handicaps. Yet most of us are not, despite our many blessings. Why is this? How are we restricting our experience of life? This chapter explores some of the ways we hold ourselves back and offers suggestions for breaking out of the jail of our limiting minds.

As children we are told, "No, you can't do that." Our energy gets shut down until our natural spontaneity is squelched into conforming submission. We were constrained, but we can bust back out! We can unleash the brilliant force of spirit that we are by giving up the limitations we accepted as children. We do that by dropping our excuses, complaints and judgments, and by letting go of our addiction to our suffering so that our spirit can grow and blossom. Then *love* becomes the doorway to our unlimited Self.

Self-talk...
One simple way to see where we hold ourselves back is to look at our limiting self-talk. When we say, 'I can't,' 'I won't,' 'I never' or 'I always', we have constructed beliefs about ourselves that we think are real. If we disconnect from those beliefs we can find verbiage that leaves us open to new possibilities. We could say, 'I'm finding this challenging' or 'Up until now' or 'In the past'.

Examining the way we speak illuminates our limiting beliefs. Are we constantly putting ourselves down, hooking into our program of worthlessness, or do we allow ourselves room for expansion? When we tell ourselves that we are bad/ugly/not good enough, we attract situations that validate those beliefs. Instead, we can drop into our witness to notice when these old thought habits creep into our heads. Then we simply unhook from the judging mind, allowing ourselves to remain in a place of unlimited potential. What happened yesterday is not necessarily what will happen today unless we believe it to be so.

I was the only student at my yoga teachers' training course who couldn't do a headstand. I labeled myself as 'The one who never did a headstand'. At some point during the training, I realized that I had to shift my attitude about that pose or I was not going to get anywhere with it. I could acknowledge I was having difficulty, but maintain that it was not impossible. When I changed my self-talk a miracle happened and I found myself floating effortlessly up into the pose!

Opposing our tendencies…

Doing the opposite of our tendencies is a great way to bring balance into our lives and to explore our potential more fully. If we do the opposite of what is familiar, the outcome will be different. Spirit can give us new experiences. My tendency is to move through life at break-neck speed, traveling around and engaging in a lot of social activity. To balance that, my opposite action is to stay home, slow down, cook and garden on my own. With this slowing down I experience a greater sense of peace and relaxation. The slowness balances me and I feel more present for myself and others.

My friend John lives in an ashram where the teacher encourages his students to do whichever tasks are the biggest challenge for them. For example, John is an intellectual type, hardly practical-minded. So he is given the job of handyman around the house! Or he gets to cook. His right-brained, artistic wife is encouraged to balance the house accounts! John reports that these challenges, though difficult, open him up in new ways and give him tremendous satisfaction.

How we limit ourselves…
Negative self-talk
Not being honest
Care-taking others
Judging ourselves and others
Making assumptions
Playing small
Holding grudges
Identifying with appearance
Perceived financial scarcity
Thoughts of the past
Putting someone else in a box
Having expectations and demands
Repeating the same patterns
Attaching to outcome
Playing 'safe'
Taking life too seriously
Not allowing time for creative play

Over-working

Not asking for what we want

Complaints…

A complaint is saying no to *what's so*. It's a resistance, a stand for our ego against the Creator. It's also a demonstration of our dependence on the external for our joy. Things have to be our way or we are unhappy. Most of us have an addiction to our complaints. We complain about ourselves, our friends, the weather, the dog, and above all we love to complain about our problems! We spin around and around with our complaint stories directing our energy into the problem rather than being empty enough to receive an inspired solution! Anytime we hear ourselves saying, 'It shouldn't be this way', we are in a complaint mode. Other veiled complaints are, 'I wish it were….' Or judgments such as, 'That's not good enough'. Complaints drain our energy and create contraction in the body leaving us less open to life. Understanding this makes it absurd to complain about anything!

When we accept *what's so* and are in a place of non-resistance to what is happening around us, our life flows effortlessly with fewer bumps. Things come and go but we are no longer dependent on these external events for our happiness. Fear of loss and change evaporates as we hold a state of greater and greater Presence within ourselves that gives us peace no matter the circumstance.

Money…

Our relationship to money says a lot about our limiting beliefs. There is a theory that if we were to give everyone in the world the same amount of money, in five years the rich would be rich again and the poor would be poor, precisely because of this inner consciousness of abundance or lack. One of my teachers even said that our money issues are linked so closely to our ego that if we clear them all we would be very close to waking up! The work here is to sleuth out our 'money blueprint', our patterns and beliefs about money that we inherited from our parents or absorbed through society, and change the ones which keep us from the flow of our natural abundance.

For example, many of us took vows of poverty in past lives, or even in this life. We hold the belief that having money isn't spiritual. We must release all vows of poverty, both past and present. They are no longer necessary! If we see money as the root of all evil we unconsciously block prosperity. Instead we can open to the abundance of God pouring in! It may not be cold, hard cash. It may be as simple as a friend unexpectedly treating us for lunch or finding an item on sale that we needed to buy anyway.

How we spend reflects how we feel about ourselves. *Terry never feels like she deserves the best of anything. She shops at sales to find bargains, buys used cars and the cheapest meals in restaurants. Thrift is her motto. If she does splurge on a luxury item, she feels guilty about it.* Until she is willing to examine her core issue of unworthiness, that pattern will probably not change for her and she will continue to feel a sense of financial scarcity.

Changing our spending patterns to validate our worthiness doesn't mean we need to go out and buy a Porsche or designer clothes. Small spending decisions like buying organic rather than conventional vegetables, or having the car detailed rather than cleaning it ourselves work just as well. Making new choices like these, then observing how we feel about them is a good marker of how we are doing with our worthiness program. Do we feel good about those choices or guilty?

It's never money itself that is the stumbling block but our attachment to it and beliefs about it. Many of us cling to money as a way to feel safe or valued, because we have lost the sense of our intrinsic worth. As we progress with our work of clearing the ego, we learn to trust that Spirit takes care of our worldly needs. We can be in a place of detachment and neutrality with regard to money, seeing it as a flow, surrendering any need for hoarding or fear of spending.

The following questions help us examine our fears and beliefs about obtaining and spending money:

What did our parents believe about money? Did they show a consciousness of lack or abundance?

What decisions have we made based on our parents' beliefs? How do we treat ourselves as a result?

Do we have shame and guilt about spending money on ourselves? If so, where does this come from?

Do we feel we deserve nice things?

Are we afraid of being poor? If so, why?

Do we believe that if we are rich, people will only love us for our money, or we will get lazy, or that it will create discord in the family? Or we will lose our disciplined spirituality? These beliefs set up resistance to attracting money to us.

Excuses..

Excuses are lullabies that hold us back from living fully. Are we feeling alive, ecstatic and grateful for every precious moment in life? If not, what's the excuse? What are we willing to do about it? If there is an inbuilt attachment to this excuse, what is its origin?

The first level to look at is whether or not we are experiencing our heart's delight. Are we holding off on doing what we know brings us joy and fulfillment by using excuses like age/lack of money/ kids/job security? I know people who complain that they would love to do a yoga retreat with me but say they can't afford it. Yet they think nothing of buying a daily double espresso which, in two months, would be the equivalent cost of a yoga weekend! If we really want to do something, there is *always* a way to be found, yet many of us put ourselves in mental boxes with no creative ideas as to how to escape! Normally there are some underlying fears at work that are holding us back. If we can bring these fears out into the light of our awareness and process them using the methods outlined in Chapter 7, we will feel freer to move forward with life. Then we can do what brings us joy and makes us feel alive and happy instead of feeling lost in routine drudgery that robs us of our life-force.

A deeper level is letting our current life be our heart's delight. We accept and love our life so deeply that we feel an ecstatic aliveness present within us as we take pleasure in every sensory moment. Do we have excuses for not accepting our lives with gratitude? I used to think I could not be happy and fulfilled unless wonderful and exciting things were happening. I have since found that my 'need' for stimulation was a limiting excuse. The more I remember to appreciate each precious moment there is simply no room for wanting life to be any different than the wonderful way it is, so I am always feeling joy, no matter what is happening!

One of my students brought up a contextual excuse. He said it was all very well feeling at peace with life when we sat in jnana group together, but noticed it was harder to maintain this state of openness and acceptance when he was out in the working world surrounded by less conscious people. The answer is yes, it may be harder, which is why we practice witnessing ourselves. Yet it is perfectly possible to remain conscious and aware in all circumstances.

What's the risk?

When we don't take risks we stay stuck in our box of routine and familiarity. We become dulled, uninspired and calcified. It takes courage to take a risk because we have to confront our deepest fears and limited beliefs about what is possible. Yet the rewards are great. Taking risks expands us out of our comfort zone. It also expands our comfort zone by creating different neural pathways and experiences for us that become our new known. It makes life juicy! We feel more alive. We deepen our experience of life.

Where have we held ourselves back from our maximum potential choosing security over passion? For example, our fear of rejection is greater than our desire for love so we refrain from telling someone we are attracted to them. Can we face any fear head on and do what we want to do anyway? When we risk nothing, we get nothing. *We are as free as we dare to be.*

Risks my students committed to take...
Leave a relationship
Jump into a relationship
Confront the spouse about taking financial responsibility
Taking a vacation alone
Spending money on education for a different career
Placing a personal ad
'Tooting my own horn and owning my skills'.

Examples:
I know of a Canadian student named Eileen. She had three teenage children when Spirit called her to go and study healing work in the United States. She made the choice to ignore the excuse of family obligation and follow the call. She left her husband and children for a week each month in order to study. Eventually she became a teacher at the school and left her family completely. I met one of her teenage daughters and this daughter did not feel abandoned or unloved. The connection between Mother and family was still strong and everyone was still getting their needs met. Eileen had chosen a husband who was willing and able to take care of the kids. The children were able to grow to be more independent and strong as a result of her choice. Their relationship with the father strengthened. It worked for everyone. This is a great example of how following Spirit's guidance is always the highest choice for all concerned.

Brad wanted to be an artist when he was small. His father used to discourage him from following that dream, and instead pushed him to become an engineer. Brad was fed the idea that a 'sensible' job would pay the bills and keep him safe and secure. Now in his fifties, Brad is still an engineer and hates his job. He had felt compelled to continue in this unfulfilling work. When we looked at his excuses for not leading a joyful life, Brad recalled his father's words loud and clear and realized this was his excuse for not living out his life's dream of becoming an artist. He was driving someone else's car, not his own! Now that he has seen this clearly, Brad is preparing to change his career.

I was practicing partner yoga with Kevin, a new student. We were both in a squat and he said, "I can't hold this position any longer." So I invited him to look into my eyes and focus on my gaze. He did—and completely forgot about his aching calves and complaining attitude! We both dropped into a timeless state of Presence together and he said he could have held the pose for hours after that!

Exercises:
1. Make a list of:
   "I believe that if I am rich...." (fill in the blank).
   Then offer the list and its contents up to Spirit with a prayer for healing.
2. Think about something you've always wanted to do, but not done, both on a daily basis and a one-off basis, such as a big trip. What are your excuses for not doing those things?
3. What talents have you suppressed? If you knew you could not fail which dream would you pursue right now? Make a step toward doing one of them! Or just do them!
4. Observe the complaining mind. Every time you hear yourself complain, follow it with an appreciation.
5. With a partner: Discuss where you have been holding back from doing something you would like to do. Why have you done this? What might you gain by taking the risk to do it?

4.
HOW CAN I FIND BALANCE?

The science of yoga is about achieving balance and raising our frequency so we can experience union with the Divine. We practice jnana yoga and meditation to clear the mind, hatha yoga to balance the body and karma and bhakti yoga to awaken the heart. These practices help bring us into balance, a neutral state beyond the pull of polarity and duality where mind, body and spirit are in harmony. When we are in balance we can cope with undesirable situations more gracefully. We are grounded in our core and nothing disturbs our peace.

My type 'A' personality has given me the tendency to be an over-achiever. I do, do, do….and go, go, go, burning my energy high and bright, which worked when I was younger and more resilient; but now if I do this, my body rebels. My adrenals burn out and I am prone to illness. Getting sick is my body's attempt to balance the activity with a quieter state of being. It's not a very gentle way for me to find balance. It takes its toll on me physically. As a consequence, I have learned to pay attention to my need to balance my energy and take time to just 'be' whenever possible.

When we are in balance we surf the waves of life. Whether they are gentle little rollers or big crashing whoppers, being in our center allows us to stay on our surfboard and ride the wave, no matter what. Everything passes through us easily as though we are transparent. Nothing sticks. We are at peace.

Our energy bank…
I have a friend who works in the corporate world. He gets up at 5:00 a.m., grabs a Starbucks latte en route to work, sits in traffic for an hour, works a ten hour day, comes home, eats fast food for supper then collapses on the couch. He stays up till 1:00 a.m. surfing the net and playing video games, then gets up the next day and does it all again. He is exhausted and unhealthy and knows he is out of balance. This lifestyle has caused him to have heart problems, resulting in a heart bypass operation. He is way overdrawn on his energy bank account.

When energy is moving into us, we are in a 'yin' or receptive aspect of being. We can call this our feminine state. When energy is directed out from us towards the world, we are in the masculine or 'yang' state. It's a useful exercise to think about our regular day and see what percentage of time we spend in each of these states. In this culture, very many of us notice that the yang state is the dominant one. We have so much to do, so many things that need our attention that our energy is constantly being drained. Is it any wonder we are stressed, sick and tired a lot of the time?

We can practice balance on a daily basis. Overworking and being stressed out all year and then taking a week's vacation drinking ourselves into oblivion in the Bahamas doesn't serve us! Neither does partying hard on the weekends in an attempt to balance the stresses and rigors of the week! However both are unconscious draws towards finding some balance in our world. We *do* need to recharge our batteries but there are healthier ways of doing it.

If we have the tendency to be too yang with our energy, meditation and gentle hatha yoga practices are great ways to draw energy back in. We get nurtured by Spirit and uplifted with light, replenishing ourselves for being in the world again. In our jnana group we came up with some other ways, such as gardening, journaling, napping, playing music, being in nature, breathing deeply and saying no to extra commitments.

If our tendency is to be too yin, a healthy way to balance this would be to offer our services in some way, so that we are extend our love and energy to help others. We could volunteer for an organization or mow the neighbor's lawn.

Balancing the body...

So often we take our health for granted—until something goes wrong. Then, often dramatically, our bodies become the most important focus of our attention. When a health challenge occurs we often berate ourselves for not doing what we know we should for optimum health. The good news is we can change our unhealthy patterns and habits! What are we prepared to let go of to commit to better health now? If we take care of our physical body and give it the right amount of exercise, the correct blend of food and adequate rest we can stave off the disease that happens when we are out of balance. In so doing we honor the body as our sacred gift. If we treat it well, it will take care of us.

When did we last get a physical tune-up? We tune up our cars and change the oil regularly, so why not our body? Bringing the body into balance is the basis for the science of acupuncture, where the yin and yang energy flows of the body are either stimulated or calmed down. Herbal cleanses are available to clean out toxins from vital organs. Hatha yoga is like having acupuncture from the inside out. It balances us physically and mentally. As we tune into our body's natural frequency, we will be led to the practitioners and practices that will help us uncover our own vibrant health.

Then there is the great food debate. The only piece of solid advice I can give here is to get good personal recommendation from a trained naturopath or ayurvedic doctor! Everyone has a different blood type and constitution. Diet is an individual thing. Food can be either medicine or poison and it is vital that we all know what is balancing for us to eat. Generally it is better to eat unprocessed, organic food. Raw, live food is great if you can tolerate it, or steamed vegetables in abundance. Are we getting our 'five a day'? Are we taking time to eat and enjoy our meals with good company or are we gulping down our food on the run or in the car?

Our jnana group looked at resistances to eating right. Many people work long hours and live alone. They felt it was just too much effort to shop and cook for themselves. It was easier to stop at a fast food place and grab a quick bite. The solution we came up with was to start a supper club. We divided into groups of six and on a given Wednesday one of us would cook for the group. This was fun. It created a greater sense of community for us and we all got to eat a healthy home-cooked organic meal at least once a week!

When I asked my group how many of them felt that they got adequate rest less than a third responded affirmatively. Many of them said they watched TV or surfed the web just before going to bed, which left their minds busy and unable to shut down. Some cited the evils of caffeine too close to bedtime. Those that did get enough sleep said they were helped by drinking chamomile tea or hot milk before bed, taking passion flower capsules, listening to inspiring soft music or reading. Above all, what helped encourage a good night's sleep was feeling at peace with the day by releasing any grudges, letting go of stresses and clearing the mind of worries.

Beyond getting enough sleep, just having quiet, restful days seems to be a challenge in this high-pressure world. With their monthly cycle nature has given women a regular reminder to slow down and take care of themselves. The native American women of old would gather in the 'moon lodge' when their monthly cycle occurred, so they could be together and just do NOTHING but nurture themselves! We have medications for the pain so we can carry on regardless! But what is the price we pay for this? Can we love ourselves enough to prescribe quiet, restful days whether or not we are sick?

With the ever-challenging issue of getting motivated to exercise, our group decided that exercising together and making it fun was the key. In Sacramento, we have a wonderful bike trail that stretches for thirty miles along the American River. One member of the group, Jonathan, took it upon himself to organize a weekend bike ride. Many people participated and now it has become a regular event. Others have formed a hiking group and some meet and go dancing together.

The brain…

Finding balance between the left and right sides of the brain is essential if we wish to access higher consciousness. Since early school days our minds have been trained to think logically, which makes most of us use our left brain. Our left brain is our masculine side. It is responsible for our logical thought, reasoning ability and organizational faculties. It is the body's data processor and thinks in a linear, sequential fashion.

Our right brain is the feminine side, the source of our creativity, inspiration and artistic talent. It is holistic and intuitive. Women have evolved to have a greater capacity to function from both sides of the brain, hence the phrase 'womens' intuition' and the female propensity to have greater access to feelings and emotions. Men are often functioning only from the left brain. That's why they are so good at mechanical things and at finding solutions for problems.

One easy way to balance the brain mechanically is walking. The motion of using one leg then the other helps us balance. Is it any wonder we often get filled with great ideas when we are out for a stroll? Then there is the ancient yogic breathing technique of *aniloma viloma*, or alternate nostril breathing (see description below). Other ways to bring the brain into balance are cycling, standing on our heads, rhythmic breathing, Tai Chi, or hatha yoga. We can also practice using our non-dominant hand for writing or other activities, such as gently brushing the teeth.

It's a good exercise to look and see which part of our brain we are using the most. Many of us overuse the left side of our brain. To balance this we might want to do activities that encourage the use of the right brain, such as art, dance, poetry, music, needlepoint, yard-work, sweeping, doing massage, chanting or laughing. If we are the type of person who tends to daydream and get 'spacey' we may be spending too much time in the right brain. Then we would need more left brain activities for balance. We could make checklists, do mathematical puzzles, balance our check book, do computer work, or fix a car engine. Anything that requires us to be focused and organized!

Alternate Nostril Breathing:

1. Cover the right nostril with the right thumb and inhale through the left nostril.
2. At the top of the inhale, retain the breath a moment.
3. Cover the left nostril with the ring finger and exhale through the right nostril.
4. Inhale through the right nostril, retain a few moments again, then exhale through the left nostril, covering the right nostril with the thumb again.
5. Repeat a few times.

The mind...

In our daily waking activity our minds are constantly busy with thoughts. We plan, evaluate, organize, create and interact. Meditation balances this activity of the mind. It allows us to drop our relationship to time as we rest in timelessness. We recharge our batteries and are refreshed for the rest of our day. The mind has been empty and quiet and now it can be alert and ready for what is next.

There are many techniques for meditation. Some people use a mantra to help quiet the mind. If we don't know one, we can use the mantra 'om' or 'peace' or 'thank you'. Other methods focus on watching the in and out flow of the breath. Personally I like to use guided meditations and to meditate to soothing music. It helps my mind to relax.

In meditation, we find our center by focusing on our *sushumna*, the Sanskrit word for the core of light that runs from our perineum up through the energy body to the crown of our head. This is our God-light, our connection to the Divine. When we focus our attention here our energies come into balance and the mind becomes quiet. We are fully aware yet our minds are completely still.

In jnana yoga we balance the mind by using our witness to observe our thoughts. Witnessing helps us to take a step back and disconnect from believing that each thought is anything more than the mind at work. Through this observation we allow thoughts to come and go without taking them seriously. The more we witness ourselves, the deeper we drop into conscious awareness where the mind can take a back seat to the Presence that we are.

Our ego-centric universe...

The purpose of the ego is to create an internal self-centered world. Its voice says, "me, Me, ME. *My* process, *my* challenges, *my* triumphs, *my* awakening." It can get very tiring. To find balance with this we can do something to take a

31

break from ourselves—by focusing on others instead! This is the path of karma yoga, selfless service to others with no attachment to outcome. We give to others for the sake of being of service, not because we are getting paid, or might win approval or earn cosmic brownie points. We give because we have a desire to serve with a pure heart. When we focus on what others need and give ourselves to that, our heart opens. We feel revitalized and refreshed as the energy of the universe supports our pure intent. We get a renewed sense of connection and fulfillment that comes from having done the work of God.

Continuous balancing...

The more conscious and awake we become the more balance naturally occurs within us. We balance work and play, inner child time with the serious adult, alone time with social life. As balance is cultivated we find that whatever our circumstance, our attention rests within us at our core. We rest in THAT.

Examples:

My lawyer friend Ed brings beauty into his legal offices with fountains, artwork and soft music, helping him to remember to stay in a more yin state of being despite the yang activity that is required.

It is said that the theory of relativity popped into Einstein's head while he was out riding his bike!

Marie brought balance of left/right brain into her classroom. She teaches English as a second language and played Beatles songs to illustrate certain phrases she wanted her students to learn! Music is heard by the right brain so the English words were memorized effortlessly by the students. It worked very well.

I had a stressful week. I had used my left brain to the point of exhaustion. Then I spent three days in the woods with a yogi friend practicing yoga, hiking and sitting quietly in Presence. My mind became balanced and settled again. When I got home my work flowed. Tasks I had procrastinated got done effortlessly as I got out of my own way and calmly did what needed to be done without resistance.

Exercises:

1. Journal this week on how much time you spend putting energy out and how much you spend drawing energy back in. Balance these activities the following week and write about how it feels.
2. Create a plan for balancing the body involving food, exercise and rest. Consult a natural health practitioner.

3. Highlight your meditation practice. Create a sacred place to practice and set aside a specific time each day to sit quietly. Experiment with guided tapes, music and different meditation techniques.
4. Discuss with a partner:
   How do I use left/right sides of the brain? How could I balance them?
5. Discuss with a partner:
   How much am I focused on myself and how much on others? Find a way to balance.

TRANSFORMING OUR SHADOW

Our shadow is the part of us that we have pushed into our unconscious. It contains hidden, repressed and denied aspects of our personality such as emotional urges and impulses. We are mostly unaware of it until it gets exposed by a trigger, an automatic reaction to an event. When we are triggered, a part of our shadow is projected out. We may yell, scream or cry uncontrollably as the cork pops out of our bottled up emotions and we explode with pent-up feelings. This tendency makes us afraid of our shadow and the ego spends much effort trying to control it.

When our shadow is cleansed of repressed emotion, we feel lighter as the ego lessens its grip on our spirit. We have access to our creativity, our power and excitement for life and can move towards a more expanded awareness of our Divine Selves. Indeed, the unexplored shadow places such a heavy burden on our psyche that we cannot ascend permanently into higher conscious states without unraveling it fully.

The shadow is also our program of negative emotional states such as rage, despair, fear or the killer instinct. It plays an important part of holding together the illusion of this third dimensional world. Without it we could not have matured spiritually. Exploring shadow helps us to accept and embrace these core negative feelings, noticing where they play out in our world. Ultimately we must love this part of ourselves as much as we love our lighter side. Then our hearts will stay open, whether we are feeling expansive or contracting energies flowing through us.

5.
WHAT'S THE TRIGGER?

We are driving down the road. Someone cuts us off. We immediately feel a case of road rage coming on. Waves of anger and indignation flow through us. We speed up, chase the car down and get our revenge by cutting right in front of them. We start to feel better and the rage subsides. What happened here? We just got triggered!

Why we have triggers...

When we were traumatized as children we became disconnected from part of our Soul Essence; this created a hole in our being. It's like a tear in the fabric of our energy field that leaves us with a sense of deficiency, separation and woundedness. We know there is a wound when we get triggered, when we react automatically to a situation and our emotional body feels a charge of energy running through that is uncomfortable. It could be a feeling of inadequacy, anger, grief, fear, sadness, abandonment, weakness, or jealousy. The feeling hangs on rather than passing through. In this way, recurring emotions are a guidepost for us to see where our Essence has been lost.

For example, I used to create situations in my life where I felt broken-hearted and abandoned. I realized that my 'love wound' needed attention. I traced this back to childhood when the lack of authentic communication in my family left me feeling emotionally abandoned, lost and alone. Using the techniques described in this Chapter, I used the trigger as a cue to heal that wound inside me and reclaim my Essence that was lost as a child. Now abandonment no longer shows up in my life.

Some people feel powerless and incapable in the presence of strong personalities and shrivel up when they are criticized, indicating a need to fill their 'strength' hole. Others get angry at the drop of a hat, showing an unhealed rage that may well cover up a deep hole of grief and pain. Most of us have many holes of varying depths. Our task in this chapter is to discover how we can use our triggers to uncover and heal these long established wounds.

Projection...

We project our inner movie, that is, the workings of our unconscious and conscious minds, onto the screen of the outside world. Everything is our personal egoic mirror. There is therefore a connection between our internal state and our experience of the world. What we feel on the inside is reflected on the outside in our life movie. Witnessing our movie and clearing the triggers that arise is therefore deep, necessary spiritual work. The longer we remain unaware, the more powerful the triggers become. When they are cleared, huge amounts of energy are released.

Projection is an energy stream that we send out from our core that wraps around something or someone. It deepens the holes in our own energy field, creating an energy leak. For example, if we do not feel whole and worthy, we may sit with a guru or teacher and project onto them our own worthiness, putting them on a pedestal of perceived grandeur to the detriment of ourselves. They are special and we are not. They are the authority and our inner voice is not to be trusted. This is a huge trap in the path of awakening! Any polarity will eventually turn into its opposite, so at some point we will get angry with our teacher and remove them from the pedestal where we ourselves placed them. We may even decide to leave them, rather than staying to examine the deeper core issues that are surfacing.

We must own our projections, retrieve them and integrate them to plug the holes in our Soul Essence. One way to do this is to notice if someone's behavior bothers us. We can label that behavior. *"She/he is so....."* The labeled behavior actually reflects an aspect of our own life that we have not integrated. For example, arrogant people annoy us. This indicates we are not comfortable with our own capacity for arrogance. It is a behavior that we have either inhibited or over-emphasized. This means, either we ourselves are often arrogant and judge ourselves for it, or we lack confidence and could be more assertive.

Once we have owned a projection, we can reflect on our past and ask Spirit to help us see when this behavior was first imprinted on our psyche and how it got reinforced, especially in our family of origin. Was one of our parents overbearing and arrogant, or meek and mild? Maybe we were told that we were arrogant as children and therefore went on to suppress our ability to acknowledge our best qualities. We often we judge the behavior of our parents and either emulate it or rebel against it. Owning our projections helps us become more accepting and forgiving of our parents and ourselves; an important part of our spiritual healing.

Our strategies...
We humans create cunning, clever strategies to mask the pain of our

wounding. We unconsciously spend an extraordinary amount of energy defending ourselves against feeling the depth of our holes! Most desires, addictions, temper tantrums and projections stem from this underlying cause. We believe in our coping strategies completely, reinforced by the fact that we see it is what everyone else is doing, too. The cycle continues…until eventually we realize that our strategies aren't helping. Trying to fill the hole from the *outside* doesn't work.

The classic and most common strategy that we adopt as adults is to look to a relationship to fill the holes. The pattern tends to run as follows: we feel unlovable so we find someone to love us. We feel a temporary elation and relief, yet over time it feels shaky and we begin to feel a growing sense of dissatisfaction. The relationship comes to an unhappy end. We feel unlovable again. We experience the emptiness of the broken heart. Our minds convince us that this was just the wrong person and when the 'right one' comes along all will be well! We become addicted to the drug of relationship and repeat the cycle over and over.

An intimate relationship can speed up our process of healing if we remain aware. We unconsciously attract partners into our lives that can best help us to see where we still have holes. It's our partner's job to trigger us! They act as our mirror, reflecting back to us the unhealed parts of our shadow. Our challenge is to stay conscious enough to be continually aware of this reflection and to take *responsibility* for it rather than dropping into victimhood, blaming and complaining. We acknowledge the triggers as they arise and clear them for ourselves until the triggering behavior no longer needs to show up. If it does show up, it moves through us like a breeze without getting caught in our emotional web. Sometimes when this stage is reached the partner has done their job for us and the relationship ends. The invitation can then be to move on to be with new people who can trigger different parts of our unhealed shadow. Once the holes have healed enough, some relationships can deepen to levels whereby the partners can stay together and live harmoniously without the play of triggers to create unnecessary drama and conflict.

Common strategies for masking our wounds:

Avoidance—we avoid relationships so we can't be abandoned or be left broken-hearted. It's safer that way.
Staying too busy—so there is no time to feel deeply.
Humor—we laugh away our pain as a means of avoiding it.
Denial—refusal to look at ourselves and admit there is anything wrong.
Control—manipulating our world so we feel safe.

Codependence—taking care of others to cover up our own feelings of being unlovable, putting the emphasis on them, not us.

Escapism—through addictions, TV, staying isolated.

Self- abuse—for example, staying in an abusive relationship so we don't have to be alone. Abuse is better than abandonment.

People-pleasing—not daring to speak the truth in case we are left alone and no-one likes us anymore.

Preoccupation with appearance—to boost self-esteem on the surface.

Armoring—to keep ourselves safe, not allowing vulnerability.

Blame—believing that others are responsible for how we feel.

How to fill the holes...

When we are triggered, the first step is to be aware that we have been assisted in our spiritual development. We celebrate the fact that in a part of our ego/mind system, our buttons got pushed! We can feel compassion for ourselves and love our triggers from our hearts, as they remind us that there is a wound for us to heal—and it's right in our face!

The process to fill in our holes starts when we take full responsibility for the trigger and we stop projecting anything onto the other person involved. It has nothing to do with them! They were only the blessed catalyst, the messenger from God, inviting us to look at our own wounding. When we see this clearly, we know that whatever they did was for us, not against us and we can thank them, even though they themselves may have no awareness of the part they played!

Then we look at the part of our shadow self that is being highlighted, such as unhealed feelings of betrayal or abandonment. We spend a moment breathing deeply, feeling into the emotion that is being brought out by the trigger. We can ask the emotion what it needs or wants and if it has a gift for us. In this way we can dialogue with our wounded part to see what insight it can give us. We then ask Spirit to take us back to the origin of this wound. We allow memories to arise, noticing how old we are and what is going on. We can let our wounded child speak to us and ask what s/he needs to heal this wound too.

Once the dialogue feels complete we ask the Divine to help us release any wounded energy that has been carried in our cellular memory. We take some deep breaths and breathe those old energies out. Then we ask for light to fill us, for the Divine to bring back that Essence that was lost. We spend some moments resting again in our own precious Presence, noticing the difference in our energy field after this healing. We may feel an emptiness, a spaciousness, a sense of greater acceptance for the way it is.

Here is the procedure in a nutshell:

1. Identify projection for what it is. Use it as an opportunity to deepen awareness of the wounded self.
2. Remember the person we are resenting is exhibiting this behavior for our benefit. God is for us, not against us, so we can be grateful for the experience.
3. Ask which part of shadow this trigger is illuminating, e.g., betrayal, abandonment, fear of loss.
4. Ask Spirit to take you to the origin of this wound. See what enters your awareness in the form of memories.
5. Integrate this aspect of shadow using inner child dialogue.
6. Ask Spirit to help release the cellular memory of the wound. Take some deep breaths.
7. Ask the Divine to bring your spirit back to fill the hole.

It is also extremely useful to continue processing the core issue by doing the squares technique as shown in Chapter 7: this will help release and balance the unconscious energy we store around the issue in our minds. If we feel courageous, we may want to speed up the process by asking the Divine to show us more of our unhealed holes. We state we are available to fully experience the wound and ask to feel it fully. Often the Divine will oblige here with an event perfectly suited to trigger us so we can see the next hole that needs our attention.

Or we can ask for a shattering...

The ultimate trigger...

The ultimate trigger is when a major event happens such as divorce or bereavement, which deals a huge blow to our emotional body. We experience grief, loss, abandonment, shame or anger to such a degree that our lives are temporarily shattered. We may lie in bed for hours at a time, unable to move. Our mind can't think. We are overwhelmed with feelings or confusion. This process can reveal aspects of our humanness we didn't know were there, dismantling our structural illusions. It is an enormous opportunity for the dissolution of the false self and allows for a reorganization of our energy to take place. Such chaos has the potential to bring about radical change. Our armor is shattered, our defenses crumble and we get to taste the very core of who we are.

My friend Jim got divorced, changed residence and met me all in the space of two months. He was retired and did not have to work. He had asked God to give him the experience of his Divinity. He was ripe for a shattering! One day he got triggered by something small that started a big process within him. I sat there with him as he got in touch with deep grief he had held for a very long time. He went into a past-life memory of being persecuted for being a speaker of Truth. He relived the pain and anger from this time and screamed it all out. After that he felt like he no longer knew who he was. Like swimming in a void, he felt the terror that happens when part of the ego-self shatters and dissolves. It felt like a form of death, yet he stayed in it. He had created plenty of free time for himself, so he could let the process run its course and be present with it as long as he needed to. He came out a different person, sure of his Self and with a new strength.

We have a choice here. We can resist a shattering and numb ourselves against it by the usual strategies such as drinking, drugs, movies, being busy, work, food, or we can embrace it and allow it to take its course. This can take time. My grief at feeling abandoned took six months to process through. We are often dysfunctional at these times and need support from friends, family and associates. Yet as we emerge from what appears to be a tunnel of darkness, we glow with a new light. We are softer, more available and compassionate, and eventually our joy returns.

How we know when we have healed the issue behind the triggers...

We know when we have filled in the hole when the universe stops presenting us with the same old triggers. We no longer need them as a prompt to our healing! For example, we may have consistently attracted people who criticized us and made us feel inferior. When we have completely healed this wound the universe no longer serves us situations that trigger that emotion, so those people either stop the criticisms or they drop away from our lives. If we do hear a criticism, we are no longer triggered and hardly notice it!

For years I tried hard to keep safe by avoiding partnership situations where I would feel triggered by jealousy or fear of loss. Yet I would continue to attract situations where my jealousy would surface. When my witness felt strong enough I knew I was ready to face these demons once and for all. So the universe obliged, bringing me a man with the unique ability to trigger each of these wounds in rapid succession. This time I stayed present to my feelings and did not try to run away. I told him when I was triggered and how it felt. He knew the wounds were mine and did not try to rescue me or make me feel better. On the contrary, he sat with me and helped me discover the origin of each wound. We worked with it and cleared it. Now I am free of those particular wounds. Interestingly, the behaviors my partner did to trigger the experiences have not repeated themselves.

The universe will test us. An event occurs that in the past would have pushed our buttons deeply, but now we no longer feel the emotional charge. This is a sure sign that our Essence (Spirit) is back! The more we feel Essence the less we feel reactive emotions. We feel sensations but their quality is different. Where we used to feel anger, we now experience strength. Where we used to feel inferior, now we experience the value of our Presence. Energy from others passes through us like light through a clear pane of glass, leaving our own energy field undisturbed as we remain grounded and centered.

Meditation, where we drop back into a timeless, empty state, unidentified with the thoughts of our personality, is another great way to connect with Essence. Meditation allows light to penetrate deep within us, filling in the cracks and corners our awareness may have overlooked. When we meditate along with practicing the processing techniques outlined in this chapter, we accelerate the filling of our holes. We feel whole, centered in all situations and better able to handle whatever life presents.

Examples:

Rachel's father left her at age four. She has abandonment issues. She is in constant fear of people leaving her—friends, lovers, children. When they do, she dissolves into shattering. It hurts her very much as that old wound gets reactivated. She used to attract situations to herself constantly where she was the one who would be left alone. Eventually she developed her witness enough to be able to see that *she* was the common denominator in these situations and that maybe the universe was trying to tell her something! She started to look at her abandonment wound and process her inner child. She fills herself with her own Essence in meditation when abandonment comes up. Now she notices that the triggers are arising less frequently as she heals that part of herself.

My friend Mary is a lawyer for abused children. She was assigned to a court where the judge was known to be cantankerous and angry. An older man, he got upset easily and yelled at my friend over the slightest thing. In this situation she could not just up and leave and desert her clients. She had to stay put and deal with this angry judge, even though it left her feeling emotionally devastated inside. She realized her buttons were being pushed and needed some insight on how to handle the situation. We looked at her wounding and found that the trigger could be traced back to childhood when her father would yell at her and she couldn't escape his wrath. She would crumble and collapse emotionally just as she was doing now with the judge. We let her inner child dialogue with her father until she could feel strong again. This processing turned out to be the biggest gift for Mary. It helped heal and clear her relationship with her father and then in court she found her emotional body was no longer triggered by the angry judge. She could even be grateful to him for his role in her own process.

Craig's roommate was really beginning to irritate him. She left dirty dishes in the sink, played loud music late at night and to cap it all, vacuumed her room at 1:00 a.m., abruptly waking Craig up. Craig felt she was inconsiderate. He, on the other hand, bent over backwards to consider others, often to his own detriment. Craig realized he was being triggered and asked for my help. I asked if feeling dishonored was something that happened for him a lot. He said it did. No one else could live up to his standard of consideration.

I asked him to go back to the origin of this trigger, to a time when he felt dishonored as a child. Immediately he relived a memory of bring five years old and playing 'doctor' with his neighboring female playmate, also five years old. They were busy examining each other's differences when her father caught them with their pants down. He was furious and yelled at Craig to go home and never do this again! Craig felt a shock-wave of shame run through his body. Terrified of being punished for what he perceived as wrong-doing, he slunk home and hid for three days. Reflecting on this incident, Craig realized that his natural child-like curiosity had been deeply dishonored, leaving him with a gaping hole where part of his Essence had left in terror. From that moment on, he believed two things about life; that sex was bad and that he needed to be an ultra-considerate good boy, or he would be yelled at. His whole life had been affected by these beliefs. He had spent years in a safe ashram where sex was scorned and everyone was 'nice'.

We spent some time dialoguing with his inner five year-old, finding out what he needs to feel safe and giving him permission to be playful, curious and sexual. His homework was to practice honoring himself more and others less, to bring that polarity back into balance. After the sessions Craig's energy felt completely different. He came more alive, was more engaged with everyone and funny. He even started to let his naughty side out!

Exercises:
1. What strategies do you normally use to avoid feeling the pain of your holes? Write a list.
2. Which trigger has been most consistent in your life. Look for a pattern. What does it remind you of from your childhood experience? Using the process given above, dialogue with your inner child about this. Do a square around the issue (see Chapter 7 for square instructions).

3. What has been triggered in you recently? Describe a situation and how it felt, and what you projected onto the other person about how they were wronging you in some way. Which part of your shadow is screaming for healing with this?

4. Make a list of the five most important people in your life. Write their names in a row across the top of the page. Write their characteristics, your judgments of them, in a column under their name.

    Look at the list. Is there a pattern or theme? Does the theme remind you of your parents, either reflecting their behavior or its opposite? We often devalue and judge the qualities our parents had.

    Next to this list, write down the opposite word. Then offer a prayer to God to ask for healing of the imbalances in the mind.

    If one issue feels very charged, do a square with it (see Chapter 7).

5. Think about characteristics that you don't like about your partner or someone close to you. After each subject write down what that reflects about you. (For example, I don't like my partner's messy bathroom habits. On reflection, I acknowledge that I am messy too, in my closets and drawers. Seeing my projection neutralizes my intolerance and judgment of my partner.

6.
WHO'S AFRAID?

FEAR—False Expectations Appearing Real

When I was young I wasn't afraid of anything. After all, I'd pulled some pretty crazy stunts. I traveled around the third world as an adventurer, hitch-hiking alone through Southern Africa when I was only nineteen, climbing the Nepalese Himalayas and swimming with sharks in Belize. Yet this wasn't really a stretch for me. In some ways it was an escape, an escape from confronting the deeper, more painful issues of my life that involved the world of my emotions. That world *really* scared me!

We're all afraid of something. I'm afraid of not being loved and accepted. For years I was the good little girl, the straight 'A' student or the charming hostess to manipulate people into liking me so I would not have to confront this core fear. It worked. I've been loved and adored by many. I have led a neat and packaged life, but often at the cost of hiding my true feelings and concealing my authentic Self.

Origin of Fear...

Fear is our most primal human emotion. It is genetically encoded in us to help us avoid danger and pain so we can survive as a species. This instinctive fear is what creates the 'flight or fight' response that pumps adrenaline into the body and prepares us for action. This is a healthy fear, as it protects us.

But fear has evolved beyond just helping us avoid physical pain. Now we enlist it to help us avoid emotional pain. This type of fear is in the mind, an anxiety that destroys our inner peace. The fear is usually about a mythical future. Yet the body still responds as if to an immediate perceived threat, generating an adrenaline release that in turn creates stress, the big underlying killer of our modern day.

The effect of fear...

On one side of our emotional polarity is love; on the other fear. Fear perpetuates our illusion of separation and keeps us feeling isolated and alone. It is the foundation of all negative emotions, turning observations into judgments, judgments into anger and anger into violence.

Fear makes consciousness contract, our muscles tense and our energy field draw in. Our heart rate speeds up, using more energy than usual, leaving us easily fatigued and with an impaired immune system. This contracting consciousness shuts down part of our mind, leaving us running our automatic patterns. We feel out of control, helpless and vulnerable. Fear distorts how we perceive the world. Fear says we must protect ourselves and keep safe at all costs. We justify negative thoughts and acts and exaggerate potential threats, shutting down our intuitive faculties and our ability to witness.

Ironically we tend to draw to us the very things we fear the most! A female student who came with me on a trip to Mexico with me was terrified of bugs. She was the one who had a tarantula crawl on her in a taxi! If we fear rejection and disapproval, we will constantly draw to us people who reject us and disapprove of us. It's as though the universe pays attention to all the energy we invest in maintaining the fear and allows us to be 'right' about it by bringing it to us. Our worst fears are confirmed and the vicious circle continues. That's why there's nothing to fear but fear itself.

Fear wears many clever disguises. We try to hide what we're afraid of by covering it up with arrogance, specialness, bravado and a host of other behaviors. These behaviors stop us from feeling our fear. We also create strategies to mask or avoid our fears. These strategies then begin to run our lives. Yet the degree to which we are available to feel our pain is the degree to which we are able to feel pleasure. When we numb ourselves from feeling fear we can no longer access our innate joy and our lives become bland.

My friend Adam has a core fear of not being good enough. He masks it by playing out the role of the constant over-achiever. In his sixties now, he is still the go-getter business-man, terrified to stop working and have time to feel the depth and pain of his fear. He confesses to always feeling unsatisfied and has a habit of drowning his disappointments with a daily dose of alcohol. Unless he can find the courage to face his innermost fears and confess them to the people closest to him, he will continue to lead an unsatisfying life, devoid of true pleasure and intimacy.

When we are stuck in our fear we are paralyzed. It's like a rubber band wrapped tightly around us, constricting us. Our lives cannot move forward in new ways. We keep repeating the same old patterns instead of exploring our heart's delight. I hear many people say they would love to travel, but are too afraid to go alone or too fearful to go to a country where the language is not English. Yet without courage and bravery, there can be no great satisfaction. How dull would our life be if we played it safe all the time and didn't take any risks? Ask an older person what they most regret. I doubt they will reply, "I wish I'd spent more time in the office!" Regrets tend to be about things we did not try, rather than risks we took.

> ***Behaviors that overlay fear:***
> *blaming, attacking, being defensive,*
> *staying busy, restlessness, boredom,*
> *anxiety, sleepiness, criticism,*
> *making excuses, addictions,*
> compulsions, mask-wearing

Fear of death...

The terrifying mystery and fear of death is often considered our core fear. Fear of death has its root in our illusion of separation from God. We think we are separate, finite beings and our ego convinces us that death is real and scary. Indeed, for millennia religions have controlled the masses by expounding theories of eternal damnation for sinners after death. We try to avoid death at all costs and place our faith in our own ability to survive rather than trusting God and having faith in a blissful afterlife. Our consuming fear of death projected into the future stops us from living fully now. We often play too safe and our fear of dying literally sucks dry our juice for life.

Our fear of death is simply the fear of our idea about it. If we sit with someone on their deathbed, we may discover that the actual experience of their passing has the quality of incredible sweetness and lightness, a spiritual experience grounded in love and acceptance. Truth is, we all die; everything changes constantly. Coming to terms with uncertainty and flowing with a changing world is one of the fruits of a surrendered mind. If we can learn to embrace the inevitability of our mortality our whole experience of life can change into one of gratitude and fullness.

Other common fears...

Is it any wonder that people are afraid of public speaking? Not only do we risk public humiliation, but many famous speakers were attacked and killed. Gandhi, Jesus and Dr. Martin Luther King were all nailed to their respective crosses for speaking out. We have inherited a program that fears standing out in a crowd and being vulnerable. Buying into this program squelches our authentic expression and individuality.

Another major fear is the fear of being alone. We'll do anything not to feel the depth of loneliness. We watch TV, go to movies, the mall or bar, and stay in bad relationships. This fear is rooted in our belief that we are separate beings, the core egoic pattern that sustains the mirage of this world. Yet taking time to be alone can be a great opportunity for breaking familiar patterns and experiencing more fully the Essence of our true nature. Embracing alone time (all-one time) rather than resisting it with distractions allows us to listen to the voice of God more clearly, helping to dissolve our program of separation. It can be an important period in our journey of Self-discovery.

Fear of not being 'enough' creates fear of intimacy, another common fear that prevents us from being authentic and from forming healthy relationships. We are afraid that if someone else sees who we really are they will judge us negatively, so we create masks to project out an idealized self. We think this will keep us safe, yet this perceived safety is at the expense of the incomparable joy of true, authentic intimacy. This core fear also underlies our fear of rejection. We are too afraid to ask for what we want, because we are burdened with a basic conviction that we are undeserving.

Fear of loss underlies fears of scarcity, abandonment and helplessness, fuelling our resistance to change. It dissolves our trust in God's plan for us and plunges us into grief and depression when things don't go our way.

Fear of losing control and being vulnerable freezes us into rigid patterns and routines that give us the illusion of safety at the expense of living to our maximum potential. We get fixed in our attitudes and tight in our bodies. The mask we present to the world is pulled on tighter and tighter as we lock ourselves into a life of safe conformity.

If we make a list of all the things we are afraid of, we can find some core fears underlying them all. When I wrote my list it contained fear of confrontation, fear of speaking my truth, fear of aging and fear of being alone. I noticed that the core fear underlying all of them was the fear of not being loved. This fear drove my behavior unconsciously for many years of my adult life until I became aware of the fear pattern and could see its effects.

Owning up to our fears is the first step in transformation. Once we are intimate with our fears, they no longer have the same power to contract us. We can witness our fear arising like an old friend knocking on the door of our awareness, but now we have a choice: we can continue to listen to that fearful voice or disconnect from it and live with authenticity and courage.

Examples:

Alicia experienced betrayal from her father as a child. As a result, she decided that she could not trust men. Now in her adult relationships she continues to attract men who mirror that belief back to her. Her boyfriends betray her. Her co-workers turn against her. She will continue to play out these relationship patterns until she addresses her core fear of betrayal that has led to her lack of trust.

Elmer is a classical guitarist and plays in restaurants. His worst fear was that a string would break on a gig and he wouldn't have a spare. When it finally happened, only two people were watching so he finished early and joined them for a great dinner! He saw his fears were unfounded. God always takes care of him.

My friend Diandra used to live on a boat in a marina. There was a guy there who had a nice boat but was very afraid of it getting stolen or damaged. He painted it bright red and green, as his theory was that if it were a gaudy color no-one would want to steal it. Ironically, his boat was the only boat in the marina that got stolen. His fear attracted the theft.

Ian got over his stage-fright and did 'open mike' gigs at several local coffee houses. He felt elated afterwards and empowered to continue with his passion for music.

Exercises:

1. Make a list of all your fears. After each fear, write the sentence, "I am afraid of……..because………." and fill in the blanks. The second half of the sentence will help to reveal your core fears.
2. Write out the following: "When I feel scared I want to….."
3. Write a list of all the things you have avoided doing because of fear. Next to each one, write the costs and benefits of the avoidance, then consider keeping or eliminating each fear in turn.

TSUNAMI

*O*n *December 26th, 2004 I was sitting in my hammock on a beach on Lanta Island, Thailand, writing this book. The sea was normally calm and quiet. Suddenly I heard the sound of a wave. It alerted me with a crackle as it rolled across the sand. I didn't pay a lot of attention to it. I thought maybe a boat was passing. Then a few minutes later a second, bigger wave came in. This time it covered the sand and came up to the grass. A wave of terror ran through me. I KNEW a tsunami was coming! My first thought was that I might die. I acknowledged my fear of death and curiously enough, it turned into calm. I walked into my hut, grabbed my passport and money, locked the door and ran for the hills. No one else was mobilizing. I shouted to some people I saw to 'get off the beach' but no one moved. I went up the nearest hill and took a walk amongst the rubber trees.*

After about twenty minutes, I went back towards the road, wondering if I had imagined the whole idea of a tsunami. Suddenly I saw people running away from the beach toward me—people screaming, wearing nothing but bathing suits! The big wave had come in and people were terrified! We all ran higher up the hill, and waited. And waited. All night long, we sat on the hill under the full moon; about two hundred foreigners, with no where else to go and no way to get off the island.

That whole time I was in an altered state. Time stood still. Thirst and hunger left. Fear was no more. Just the witness remained, watching the situation, calming those around me. I had faced my death and accepted that if this was my day to die, then so be it. Along with that acceptance, a strange kind of energy filled my body. I felt blessed by Grace to have been spared and very sure that I was meant to be there on that hillside, in a deep state of Presence.

As day dawned, I went back to the beach and saw the devastation. The front of the beach was gone. Where there had been cute little beach bars and restaurants, now there were only stone pillars left standing. My heart felt blasted open for the Thai people and what faced them as they picked up the pieces. My bungalow was back a bit from the beach and had been spared. My possessions were unharmed. I packed up and started to make my way back to the mainland.

7.
HOW CAN WE TRANSFORM OUR FEARS?

"Fear is the root of all craziness"- Gangaji

T
he yogis say that true mastery comes when we are free from desires and fears. We feel neither attracted to nor repelled from anything. In this chapter we will explore how to create a relationship with our fears, where they can be met and transformed rather than resisted and conquered. Fear is not a dragon to be slayed. It is a stranger to be befriended. Our personal detective job is to hunt down and investigate our fears rather than suppress and ignore them. Once we are aware of our fears, they no longer have the power to run our lives. We become true spiritual warriors, fearlessly stepping forth in all our transparency and authenticity.

Facing fear…

Fear signals that we have moved away from connection to our Divinity and are identifying with the ego. It is a refusal to trust in God and our own personal intuition. We can verbally state this distrust to make it really conscious, then investigate the fear by asking, "If this happens, then what? And then what?" Often the fear can be traced back to our beliefs about death and our fear of annihilation.

My teacher used to say, "What you fear do immediately!" It's never as bad as we think when we do the thing that terrifies us! At the very least we get it over with and it becomes a known quantity! We can look and see where we are unhappy with a situation and are resisting taking action. Are we too afraid of rejection to ask the boss for a raise, or too afraid of being alone to negotiate a more rewarding relationship with our beloved? These everyday fears take up rent-free space in our minds until we face them.

We all have pervasive, core fears that control our behavior. These underlying fears require more awareness to confront because we are so used to masking them. For example, I avoid confrontation because of my core fear of losing love. I am aware of this tendency to hide behind avoiding strategies. So now when I have a bone to pick with someone and I feel my fear surfacing of the possibility that a friend will withdraw their love from me over this confrontation, I no longer put off making that phone call. I do it straight away and clear the air.

Clearing Fear...

Tracing a fear back to it origins is particularly helpful. Most fears originated from an experience in our past or childhood. An event happened: for example, our mother did not pick us up when we were hurt and crying and we felt abandoned. Our minds made up a story about this, that whenever we are hurt and wounded people abandon us. This belief continues to run our lives and we constantly recreate situations where the self-fulfilling prophecy is played out. We fear abandonment yet continually recreate it.

Once we have touched upon the source of the fear, we need to drop deeply into the pain of it. We amplify the contracted feeling inside us, allowing the fear to envelop us for a few short moments. We can ask ourselves where the fear is being stored in the body and put our hands there. Then, when we have made the feeling as intense as possible, we relax completely, dropping into the witness state. After such emotional intensity, the mind can let go and our heart energy is more accessible. We breathe love into the place where we held our fear, until we feel the fear melting.

Dialoguing with our inner child is very important when confronting old fears. We need to console, consult and love our inner child as adults. We can ask our inner child what he/she needs in order to feel assured if a similar situation arises again. This will help us to stay conscious, should a situation occur with the potential for igniting our old fear. We now have a tool of love as an ally.

Whose fear is it?

Many fears are a result of other people's belief systems, often inherited from our family of origin. My mother has a fear of spiders. So do I. My father had a fear of intimacy. I had to learn to overcome that fear. We can write a list of our top ten fears and jot down where they came from. Was the fear learned from someone else or was it a cellular experience we had as a child? Or is it a common fear held by society, such as fear of exposing the body? In our culture many people are afraid of their bodies being fully naked. It is considered shameful, yet many cultures accept nudity.

We live in a fear-based society, so to free ourselves from commonly-held fear thoughts, we must disconnect from society's belief systems. Where I live in Sacramento there is a belief that if you live here for more than a year you will get allergies. I don't believe it and have never suffered from them after sixteen years. I choose my own experience and do not buy into the reality of other people.

Being with others who do not share our particular fears is a great help. My friend Jim was very uncomfortable with intimacy and touch, yet being with our group where loving touch is practiced, he gradually overcame this fear.

Reframing our fears...

We get afraid when we think things are going to go wrong. But if we trust that everything that happens is perfection, including death, we can reframe fears into adventures and opportunities. Breathing into fear can help turn it into excitement. We can see fear as 'frozen fun' and breath unfreezes the fun! Fear and excitement are the same energy in the body. Fear is when we say 'no', excitement is when we say 'yes' to that energy.

Fear can spur us on to dive into our unknown, face challenges and overcome them. Fear has a friend called courage, which allows the human spirit to triumph and to fulfill its highest potential. A life of courage is exciting and stimulating. Anxiety no longer cripples us. Successfully overcoming fear can be pleasurable, which explains the thrill of amusement park rides and extreme sports. We feel elated afterwards, enjoying the rush of adrenaline. It raises our self-esteem and gives us juice for life.

Being with our fear can have positive side-effects. Fearful experiences focus our attention, making us feel very alive. It helps us survive by giving us intense concentration, energy and motivation. When I first bought my house I went into anxiety over money. This caused me to panic, but out of the fear came a focus and creativity that led me to think up a variety of new workshops and ways of producing income that served not just me but everyone who participated.

Fear also connects us with our humility. It helps us drop our mantle of superiority and invites us to be real with what we are feeling. In workshops, people who open up and speak from the heart are daring to be vulnerable, yet I notice that they are always more connected with the group as a result.

Mantras for calming fear...

If we've met and welcomed fear and it's still lurking in the background of the mind, another tool we can use is to chant a mantra. In India mantras are sacred Sanskrit words that hold power. For example, 'om namah sivaya' or 'jai ma' or 'shreem'. They are repeated over and over, either out loud or silently, to calm the mind, distracting it from negative emotions and opening the heart.

If chanting a Sanskrit mantra is not our cup of tea, then a simple word such as 'thank you' or 'yes' will create the same peaceful feeling.

Mantras help us to have trust and faith that all is for our highest good, no matter what happens. Trust literally eats fear for dinner!

Leslie's squares...

One of my teachers, Leslie Temple-Thurston, has given me permission to share a very powerful technique for transforming fear that she calls squares (for more details see www.corelight.org/squares). We live in a world of polarity where we are either being attracted or repelled. We have desires or fears. Once we start to uncover our core fears we can bring them into balance by using this technique. For example, one of my core fears is 'not feeling loved'. Its opposite for me is 'feeling loved'. So I make a square with headings like this:

Desire to be loved	Fear of being loved
Desire to not be loved	Fear of not being loved

Then I start to fill in the squares with whatever words jump into my head from my unconscious. Sometimes I take a week playing with a square until all the garbage is out of my head and on paper.

Once the square is complete, the next step is to offer it up to the Divine for transformation. I say a prayer, which goes something like this:

Dear God, please take my distorted thinking and bring my mind into harmony and balance. I offer my imbalanced thoughts and polarities from these squares to you for transformation. Please bring me into the neutral witness state. I thank you with deepest gratitude for your Grace, trusting these changes will be made for me.

Then I wait a minute and often have the experience of Grace descending upon me. I feel a shift in my energetic and mental state. Afterwards I feel lighter, more peaceful, and I sense that something in me has cleared.

Squares are great because they accelerate our ability to bring our dualistic nature into balance and they give our minds something positive to do about transforming fears. I have done squares for many different issues and each time I feel light coming into my being as a result of having the discipline to examine the fear.

Other good subjects for our squares practice:
- fear of being separate /desire to be separate
- abandonment/inclusion
- death/life
- abundance/lack
- rejection/acceptance
- confrontation/avoidance
- power/powerlessness
- victim/tyrant
- intimacy/loneliness
- success/failure
- feeling enough/not enough

Example of a Square:

Fear of being loved	*Desire to be loved*
Loss	Fulfilling
Grief	Cherished
Change	Intimate
Abandonment	Growth
Can't sustain it	Companionship
Vulnerable	Fun
Will lose energy	Exciting
Give myself away	Sexy
Powerless	Warmth
Stuck	Nurturing
Rut	Acceptance
	Trust
	Joyful
	Compassionate
	Fulfill potential
	Practice authenticity
Desire to be unloved	*Fear of being unloved*
Independent	Lonely
Free	Withering
Autonomous	Sad
Self-reliant	Unfulfilled
Peaceful	Lack of passion
Not vulnerable	No intimacy
Nothing to live up to	Contracting
Can't hurt	Unaccepted
Cruise in safety	Not good enough
Energy all for me	Boring
Selfish	No juice
Greed	Unconnected
	Excluded
	Rejected
	Abandoned

Substituting Presence for fear...

Ideas in our minds about a projected future are what cause anxiety. These ideas take us out of the present and prevent us from dropping into 'what's so'. Being fully present and centered does not allow room for fear, even for fear of death.

When we feel fears arising, rather than denying them or pushing them aside with bravado, we can enlist the help of our witness to be with the fear.

We invite the fear in fully and allow ourselves to express it as completely as we can. Ironically, when we do this the fear magically subsides. What's left is just Presence. If fear should arise again, we witness it, say 'hello' and disconnect from it. We are with the feeling in a detached way, knowing it no longer has power over us. Fear is only powerful when we are trying to escape it. Instead we can take a conscious breath and ask *'what's so* now'?

From fear to freedom...

We must stand up to the program of fear and see it for the illusion it is! Once we investigate our fears fully we come to realize that none of them have any validity, even fear of death. When we have realized the nature of the immortal soul, all fears lose their grip on our psyche.

The good news is that when we have cleared a certain critical amount of our fears, the remainder fall away altogether in a bundle. If we face the big ones first, the smaller ones will take care of themselves. By processing our fears as suggested here we unravel our fear program, leaving us free to flow courageously through life.

Examples:

Jan had a huge fear of being dependent on anyone else. She had seen her father admitted to a rest-home with Alzheimer's and did not want that to happen to her. She refused assistance of all kinds, playing out the desire to be independent to such a degree that she became aloof and cold to friends who offered her help. Once she became aware of her fear and did a square to clear it she was able to start asking for help in small ways, taking baby steps towards conquering the deeper fear inside. She hired a house-cleaner and asked her friends for back rubs. When she realized her friends were happy to help her and it was not a burden to them at all, she relaxed and the fear began to dissolve.

As a child, Don was ridiculed and rejected by his peers. He grew up with low self-esteem and a huge fear of criticism and rejection. In order to avoid rejection, he rejected people first, building a wall around him that seemed impenetrable by anyone. One year he came to Mexico for an intensive with my group. I have a very loving group of students who like to do this trip and they were not going to let him get away with isolationist behavior! We encouraged him to admit his fear, then open to the possibility of a different experience. After a few days he let down his guard and was well and truly assimilated by the group. He said that for the first time ever he felt included, accepted and loved by a group. Now he has a new model of the universe in which to experience the rest of his life.

I know someone who used to be afraid that his new car would be damaged in some way. He realized that being attached to this desire for perfection was costing him energy and aggravation. So now when he buys a car he immediately takes a coin and scratches the paint so he can let go of any desire for the car to remain perfect!

Exercises:

1. Pick a fear and confront it head on! Do it immediately!
2. Pick a core fear and do a square for it. Offer it up to Spirit for clearing.
3. Write in your journal: 'If I wasn't afraid I would...'
4. Choose a core fear to clear. Dive into feeling this fear while holding your forehead and the back of the neck. This occipital holding helps to release the trauma stored in the nervous system. Intensify the feeling of fear. Feel it fully. Feel where it is stored in the body. Does it have a color? Trace this fear back to its origin, in childhood. See the event where it started. Dialogue with your child about it. Ask the child what it needs in future in order to feel safe when this fear arises. Now breathe the energy of love from your heart into the place where the trauma is stored. Allow the love energy to dissolve the trauma.

8.
WHO'S ANGRY?

"When we don't accpet a fact, we create what we call a problem." Paul Lowe

Imagine this...as little children we are born into the world. We are hit and made to cry. If we are male our foreskin is cut off with no anesthetic. As we grow older we are told, "Be quiet, don't cry and be good." In short, we are asked to conform into what often feels like an alien world. Parents, school and society deny the expression of our authentic Self. We are frustrated. Our sense of personal power is denied. Is it any wonder we are angry?

Anger often overlays a variety of other feelings such as frustration, resentment, grief, shame or fear. It's a strategy for covering up these deeper feelings that can make us feel powerless or weak. The expression of anger helps us feel powerful again as we raise our energy by venting and raging. Most of us learned this behavior as a child. When we were frustrated we would yell and stomp until we got what we wanted. Showing anger became a way to control others around us.

Society teaches us to control anger, not transform it. In control we repress; in transformation we express. This suppressed anger makes us violent people. We eat, breathe and live violently. The anger poisons our food, our love and eventually our organs. We become afraid of our own anger and of losing control so we push it down with masking strategies, denying our authentic Selves and our true passion. We become numb and rigid.

The nature of anger...
Anger is like a bolt of electricity moving through us. It is a hot energy; hence the expressions 'hot under the collar' or 'hot-headed'. This inner heat creates an energy within that demands immediate release, tempting us to lash out at the person we perceive has 'made us angry'. Yet the expression of anger need not be directed at anyone. If we throw it at someone else we initiate a chain of reactions and enemies are created. Anger is mental vomit. If we need to vomit we go to the bathroom. We don't vomit over someone else!

We try to control others with our anger, to instill fear so that we get our own way. We intimidate and use theatrics. This is the expression of the archetype of the tyrant who attracts victims on whom to perpetrate these patterns of abuse. Yet beneath all tyrants live cowards, often using anger as a cover-up for their own fear.

The cost of anger...

Repressed anger drains our luminosity and energy. It keeps us from our joy, from loving others and from self-compassion. It shuts the heart down, our sensitive core. People avoid us when we are angry because we can be out of control, aggressive and hostile. We blame everyone except ourselves for our situation, refusing to take responsibility. We stub our toe on the couch and yell at the couch. People are fearful of our aggressive behavior and withhold their love from us, leaving us isolated and even angrier.

Most violent and abusive acts have anger as their source. Anger blows up inside of us like a balloon and becomes rage. When it is too full, it bursts and we explode into a tantrum. This rage is the source of barroom brawls, child abuse, road rage and even obsessive muscle building at the gym.

Anger at God...

Anger at God is built into the human ego because of the soul's experience of our original separation. We don't want to be here. We resent our families or our situation. We feel like a victim, like someone put us here on the earth against our will. We are angry that we are suffering. Like aliens stranded on a foreign planet we feel that 'home' is someplace else.

If we persist in harboring anger at God, on an unconscious level we may create ways to check out. Near-death experiences, accidents, insanity or illnesses may happen. This anger can be resolved through venting. We can do this alone without involving anyone else. We can scream obscenities at God, yell at our misfortune to be cast away on this planet and generally let God have a piece of our mind! Anger fills the chasm that exists between God and us so until we have released this anger we will continue to uphold our sense of separation. This is not a piece of work that can be done intellectually. We must clear our emotional body of these deep, core feelings of anger before the chasm can knit together.

Once we have released our anger we can realize our own Divinity. We recall that our suffering is caused only by our thoughts and not by God. We accept that we are responsible for our choices and our responses to life, no matter our situation. On some level we have volunteered to be here. Now we can forgive ourselves, forgive God and restore our spiritual connection.

What to do about anger…

When anger arises we are faced with a choice in how to respond. The automatic reaction is to lash out, which could lead to violence. Or we can take a step back, witness ourselves experiencing anger and consciously examine our response choices with awareness.

There are different ideas on how to best deal with anger. *Buddhists* advise walking away from the scene and pondering what is being triggered in us. When the emotion has died down enough for us to be able to talk calmly and with respect to the person that made us angry, we can discuss the issue without blame or violence. In this approach we separate the energy of anger from the issue. We move the anger energy through with our own internal witnessing process by going within and reconnecting with our changeless, eternal Self.

However, many of us do not have enough witnessing experience to find that quiet place within during the emotional heat of a bout of anger. The solution of *modern therapy* is to beat pillows or punching bags to move the pent-up anger energy in the body out of the cellular memory. We raise our hands high over our heads, opening up the frozen heart as we smash our baseball bat or fists down on the pillow or mattress. We can throw a temper tantrum on our own and scream and shout, or place a towel in our mouths and scream into it. Thrashing and yelling in this way unleashes stored anger energy to the outside world. We see the violence contained in it clearly externalized in a way that harms no one, yet moves the energy out. It allows the anger a healthy expression.

I know a therapist who will not work to heal anger with her clients unless they commit to doing a liver cleanse. The liver is the organ that stores our repressed anger. Going to a health food store and buying a liver cleanse herbal preparation is highly recommended to support anger release work. Over a period of two to three weeks the herbs act to help the liver release toxicity. Anger is released along with the stored toxins in the tissues.

After the physical release we investigate the source of the anger. We can sit quietly and drop into the feeling of anger, meeting it with our awareness. We can ask Spirit to show us where our anger trigger began and revisit specific incidents that pop into our minds. We look to see where we were denied free expression of our soul and grieve that lost expression. We may discover repressed feelings from the past that have fuelled our current anger. Where do we feel it in our bodies? Are we using it to avoid feeling hurt, afraid or sad? Spending a moment in dialogue with the anger, with our hurt inner child or our perceived abusers is helpful to facilitate further release.

The *path of yoga* invites us to address anger as spiritual beings. Using the witnessing approach of, 'I am not this anger', the anger dissolves in the light of our consciousness and does not get stored in the body. We let go of any story around it, no longer identifying with the emotional body's pain. This detachment releases us from the destructive pattern of our need to react and act out our anger. We give up the game. We see it clearly as an emotion that is just passing through us. We meet the anger in stillness and this stillness devours it.

My feeling is that all three approaches are useful. When we create a safe container for our anger, free from blame, we can express ourselves kindly and compassionately. If anger is an entrenched pattern and shifting our reaction mechanism is still difficult we can pray for our anger to be transmuted by asking our guides, spirit helpers and God to assist us.

When others get angry...

The number one rule is to not take other peoples' anger personally! It's their anger, not our issue! We can see this as a great opportunity to test ourselves. When someone gets angry with us, do we react and engage our ego, or listen to the person's masked pain and fear with compassion? There are different strategies on how to respond depending on our perceived consciousness of the person who is angry. If they are hysterical and out of control, self-preservation dictates the need to back away and refuse the abuse. We let go of the need to engage with them and be right or get the last word. There is no point trying to reason with the inflamed ego. Most tyrants want a victim, not a rescuer in their personal drama.

However, if the person is open we can acknowledge their feelings and ask what they really want from us. If we know the person to be very conscious we can hold a space for their anger, acknowledging it and reflecting it back so they can see it clearly, inviting them in a calm way to look at their own trigger. We could even assist them in discovering the source of their anger, as previously suggested.

The opportunity of anger....

Authentic anger is a legitimate, healthy feeling being expressed in the moment to communicate displeasure without hurting anyone else. It is let out and moved through with no attempt to change anyone or anything. It is nonviolent and is meant to communicate rather than to scare. It is a great cyclone that washes us clean, a great purifying force. Similar to this is assertiveness.

When we are assertive, we stand up for ourselves and ask for what we want. We create boundaries and stick to them, saying 'no' where appropriate. We create a safe container for people's interactions with us. Assertiveness is not controlling. It is clear, direct truth from one's heart.

The experience of anger is a simple emotional truth of the moment that can also be an alarm bell to help us act, move and change. Without it we might stay stuck in unhealthy situations or allow ourselves to continually be abused. Anger can be a protective force for safety and survival. For example, we are angry with a child who runs into the road.

A recurring anger trigger is an opportunity to look deeper into ourselves and heal our unseen wounds. We can ask ourselves, 'What am I really angry about?' 'Where in the body it is being held?' 'What is the loss I believe in?' 'Where do I believe I am a victim?' Listening to our still small voice within that knows the answers to these questions yields rich fodder for our process of Self-discovery.

Healed anger….
Dropping into awareness and Presence transforms the heat of anger into compassion, a divine power of God. As our awareness increases and our ego-mind is healed, anger falls away. The inner being relaxes so much that the external manifestation of anger is not necessary. An event that would have caused us to become angry is taken in only as information without need to retaliate. We may feel anger run through us like a bolt of electricity but it has nothing to stick to so it just moves through. What remains is compassion for any person involved who is not aware of their behavior.

Examples:
My friend Kate lived with an angry partner and would try to calm him down when he became angry. Eventually she came to realize she had a choice in how to react to his anger. Instead of pacifying him, she would say, "That hurts" and ask what was behind his anger. She held the space for him to examine his core issues, which the anger overlaid. She stopped taking it personally. Their communication and understanding for each other improved tremendously once she held her center in this way. Now her partner has started to investigate his anger and heal his core wounding.

One of my anger triggers is when I don't feel honored. I traced it back to my childhood when my feelings were not heard; I got used to accommodating everyone else.

I put myself last, hiding my feelings of resentment and stuffing my emotions. Nowadays when I am not honored in some way or when agreements are broken I feel this old anger surfacing. It now serves me as a reminder to speak my truth and honor my boundaries. When I do this, the anger dissolves.

Dave's father died when he was ten. Dave felt powerless to bring his dad back. It was out of his control and it felt unfair. He was angry, so he raged. The rage helped him to feel powerful, but it would surface inappropriately. As a result he pushed people away, becoming lonelier and even angrier. Once he started to witness his rage he was able to see clearly that he needed to heal his relationship with God. He vented and yelled until he had expressed his rage at God for taking his father away. Then the peace returned. He felt connected again, able to forgive God.

Exercises:

1. For thirty consecutive days spend at least one minute a day moving and screaming uncontrollably with the intention being to unleash unspecific anger stored in the body. If you miss a day go back to Day One and start the thirty consecutive days again. Concurrent with this process, undertake a liver cleanse.

2. To release pent-up anger at a partner: place a rolled-up towel on the floor and stand either side of the towel. Put a washcloth in your mouths and yell as loud as you can at each other, shaking fists and stomping feet. The only rule is that you may not cross over the towel or touch each other. When you feel finished, take the washcloths out and stand quietly looking at each others' eyes. Embrace if it feels appropriate.

3. Vesuvius exercise: stand up and yell out your anger! Move on the spot with fists shaking, tensing the body, stamping the feet—let it out! Spew and erupt like the volcano!

4. Do a square for 'desire to be a tyrant, desire to be a victim, fear of being a tyrant, fear of being a victim' (see Chapter 7 for instructions).

5. Write: 'When I get angry it reminds me of when......'
   e.g. 'the time my father yelled at me when I was three'. Recognize the early triggers and wounds that are crying for attention.

6. Write or speak verbally "I feel angry about......"
   Then affirm "I am willing to experience positive change in my relationship with......."

7. Write or speak verbally "I feel angry at myself for......"
   Then affirm "I am willing to experience positive change with myself in the area of......."

8. With a partner: Sit facing your partner. Your partner takes on the role of someone from your past. You have unfinished business with this person and feel angry at them. For five minutes, let yourself speak this anger out. You can say, "I resent you for..." You can yell at them, but do not get out of your chair! The listening partner just remains neutral and impassive. It is OK to repeat yourself if feelings are particularly strong! Then switch over.

9.
WHO'S ASHAMED?

Shame is like a mushroom—it grows in the dark.

I was five years old and had just started school. In England we had a school assembly each morning. One day in assembly I wanted to go to the toilet really badly and did not feel I could leave. It got to the point where I could hold it no longer. I peed my pants, leaving a puddle on the floor. Back in the classroom my teacher asked who had wet their pants in assembly. I was too scared to raise my hand. So she took us outside one by one to feel who was wet. I was shaking in my shoes at the prospect of getting found out. When she felt my wet knickers she slapped me, scolded me and sent me upstairs to take them off. I felt so ashamed. I knew my parents would be told and felt utter embarrassment at being judged as someone who couldn't control herself. This was the first time in my young life I recall experiencing the energy we call shame.

Shame is a created emotion, the illusion that there is something we can do that is wrong and there's no possibility of forgiveness. No matter how much we say, "I'm sorry," it's not enough. When we think someone has shamed us, we contract, drawing our energy in and hanging our tail between our legs. We shy away from risking the shame again and seek to protect ourselves, forfeiting our authentic expression and our power.

Humiliation and Embarrassment...
Most of us have experienced humiliation and embarrassment at some point in our lives, a moment when we wished the ground would swallow us up, a time when it felt like the disapproving eyes of the world were upon us and we were found to be lacking. Worse still, we were judged as evil, wrong or unacceptable. Each incident is a nail hammered into our personal coffin of worthlessness. We suspected we were bad and inferior and now we have proof. The world agrees with our self-evaluation. If the shame is bad enough it becomes a shock. A part of our spirit may actually split off from the rest of our being, in order to avoid more pain. Our wholeness is lost.

Our psyche creates strategies to avoid such a painful scenario from recurring. Some of us overcompensate. We set out to prove the world wrong by becoming the over-achiever or the one in control. We aim to be superior but when this doesn't work we swing back to feeling inferior and a vicious cycle is set up. When we have lost approval we go to huge lengths to get it back. We become people-pleasers, the good boy or girl. Our mask gets firmly placed over our authentic selves as we strive to avoid the pain of further humiliation.

Or we do the opposite. Convinced of our worthlessness, we hide and withdraw. Afraid of being beaten down by the world, we play small, not risking further vulnerability. We abdicate our power and creativity for the illusion of safety. But our plan backfires. The fearful energy sets up the pattern of victim, attracting tyrants into our world to play the role that we expect. The belief in our inherent worthlessness is confirmed. We start to develop the polarity of powerless/powerful. In the position of the victim we feel powerless. We don't want to feel that. We want to feel powerful, so we look for other weaker people on whom we can inflict a similar torture.

When he was about seven years old, Hugh used to get beaten up and humiliated regularly by boys at school. He in turn found a younger, weaker kid to pick on. He became the tyrant in order to feel the power he felt was lacking when the older boys picked on him. The victim/tyrant polarity became firmly established in Hugh's behavior.

Visualization to Heal Humiliation:
Recall the times in your life when you have felt the shame of humiliation or embarrassment. Pick the one with the most charge for you. What happened? Who was involved? How did it feel? What did you do with this feeling? Did you express it or take it inside? Where did you put it in the body? What patterns were set in place from this event? What did you believe as a result? How do those patterns show up today?

To heal it: Go back to the event again. This time imagine it as you would ideally like it to have been. Speak what you would have wanted to say. Notice the new reactions. Breathe this empowerment deep into your cells. Now that you feel safe, call back the piece of your soul that separated from you that day. Welcome that part of you back home through the crown of your head, into your body and your heart. Allow yourself to integrate and feel your wholeness once again.

Now say "I release.. (whatever pattern you identified)...." Replace it with an affirmation of a new behavior.

For example: "I release my pattern of isolating myself whenever I feel humiliated. From now on I affirm my intention to speak my feelings whenever necessary."

Shame of failure...

If we have a belief that we are worthless we create an internal saboteur whose function is to verify that we are not good enough. We have a self-image of failure that creates situations where we get to feel repeatedly ashamed about our inadequacy. We become addicted to this shame. It feels familiar.

My friend Greg had this tape running. He was a C student at school, never really achieving any academic success. In his working world he consistently started out strongly but would later sabotage himself and get fired. He felt ashamed of his failures, yet somehow comfortable with them.

Some religious ideals hold a picture of the perfect life that cannot be emulated by our own imperfect world, setting us up for failure, guilt and self-judgment. The ideal of the happy marriage is a good example.

My friend Connie was raised Catholic and in her church divorce was not tolerated. Her parents did divorce and were thrown out of their local church as a result. If the shame of that was not bad enough, Connie and her mother moved to another town and joined a different Catholic church. One day an acquaintance from the old church was visiting that town and came to the same church. When Connie's mom saw her, she whispered to the children to crawl out of the church on their hands and knees for fear that the lady would see them and spill the beans of her being a divorcee to the new priest. Connie carried that humiliation in her back. She developed scoliosis, as her body attempted to round over and make herself smaller so as not to be visible. Such was the weight of the shame. The energy of victim coupled with unhealed shame drew the same pattern back into her life. Years later, when she got divorced herself, she felt so ashamed that her marriage had failed that she did not even tell her own family for years.

Shame was designed to immobilize us, freezing us into patterns of contraction. We start the thaw-out process by becoming familiar with the contraction and giving ourselves permission to feel it fully, noticing its effect. Then we write a list of all the times we have felt the shame of failure. If we can identify a pattern, we can work with our internal saboteur (see Chapter 1). We forgive ourselves for past actions, seeing that we did the best we could at the time, and stay alert to our sabotaging tendencies.

Body shame...

All of us, even the most beautiful people, have body parts that we dislike. Our thighs have cellulite, our skin is too pasty, we are fat, our lips are too thin. We grow ashamed of these body parts, wishing to hide them away or at least disguise them from judging eyes. I can remember wanting plastic surgery for my ski-jump nose around the age of fourteen. I would spend hours in front of the mirror obsessing on how best to disguise what I perceived as an imperfection.

At some point we conclude that our bodies are not OK. They do not match our image of the perfect model. We feel defective, unworthy. It is useful to look back and see why this happened. Did someone else criticize us and make us feel that way? Or was it peer pressure at school and the images from magazines that led to this belief? Loving our bodies just the way they are is a must if we are to feel fully whole.

How do we feel about nudity? Do we turn the lights out before we undress in front of someone? Going to a nudist beach for a day and allowing others to look at our naked body can be scary but ultimately very healing for those of us with body shame. Where I live in California we have many hot springs resorts where clothing is optional, and nearly everyone chooses to be naked in the pools. I have brought many friends there, even my mother! Some have had a lot of fear of being seen and judged. Yet once they are there and they realize that no one is staring at them, their fears melt away and a new level of self-acceptance for their own body happens. With nudity we can feel free and natural, without clothes to hide behind. We present ourselves to the world just as we are.

Sexual Shame...

Sexuality is fertile ground for shameful thoughts and feelings. Even as we grew up, many of us absorbed negative attitudes towards sexuality as our families passed their own shame on to us. We have been shamed for masturbating, embarrassed by having an erect penis or erect nipples in public, and judged ourselves as lacking during sex. Most of us have felt sexually inadequate at some time or another. We judged ourselves for coming too fast (for men), coming too slowly (for women), having too small a penis or breasts, or not knowing how to touch. Because of the sensitive nature of these issues we often do not discuss our shame and our sexual fears with anyone. We try not to think about them and hope they will go away. Yet even these beliefs must be healed if we are to come into wholeness and accept ourselves fully.

When I was thirty-seven years old I contracted genital herpes. I was devastated. I thought my sex life was over. I felt dirty, ashamed and embarrassed about this socially unacceptable disease. Ironically, it turned out that getting herpes was the doorway into a more complete sexuality for me rather than the end. I read Louise Hay's book, "You Can Heal Your Life" and saw that herpes was about shame. "Funny," I thought. "I don't have any shame." How wrong I was. Little by little, the floodgates of my memory started to open and long-forgotten incidents came pouring in.

At nineteen, I was date-raped twice in the course of six months. In both cases I felt somewhat to blame. I felt I should have known better than to put myself in a vulnerable situation. A shameful feeling of being 'unclean' prevailed. I was terrified I would get pregnant. Luckily I did not.

Also at nineteen, I had sex with a much older man who convinced me I was frigid. Looking back it was more that he was lazy and inept. But his criticism rang in my ears and I believed him. It gave me the idea that I was lousy in bed.

A few years later a boyfriend told me that he thought I wasn't made right. There was something wrong with my genitals. Oh, the horror! For years I thought this was true and would not let a man look at me.

I tell you this, dear reader, not because I want to shock you, but because I want to be an example to you of full disclosure. In my experience, sharing these incidents with others is what has helped me to heal them. Now they no longer have a charge for me. I have been able to release the old beliefs about any perceived inadequacies. I know that I am perfect just the way I am and there is nothing wrong with me! In fact, uncovering the Pandora's box of my shame got me curious about sexuality and led me to the path of tantra, which I now teach.

In tantra yoga we have many different exercises that are used to bust our sexual shame to smithereens. If we have a partner, we may start by getting playful with a striptease, to encourage feeling good about our bodies. Then we can take turns allowing our genitals to speak, with our partner as the loving witness. In this exercise we allow our vagina or penis to tell its life-story. Then we can masturbate in front of our partner, with our partner lovingly supporting us by breathing with us and keeping eye contact. For more details on these exercises and others see "The Art of Sexual Ecstasy" by my tantra teacher, Margo Anand.

More than anything, I recommend setting up a sacred time to share your sexual history and hang-ups with a group of compassionate friends or with a loving partner. Tell them the secrets you have not told anyone. Spill out your shameful past, until it no longer has a hold on you. Then you can be free to enjoy and share the God-given gift of your body.

Transforming Shame…

Pushing shame away doesn't work. Like other emotions, it is there to serve a purpose, to keep us safe, or help us behave appropriately. The problem is that we allow the contracted feeling of shame to engulf our emotional body and shut out our spirit, leaving us feeling disconnected, unworthy and powerless. It is a great exercise to talk directly to the shame, see where it lives inside of us and ask what its job is. Then get its agreement to change jobs. As responsible adults it is our job to keep ourselves safe and behave appropriately. The shame can be transformed into a beacon of sensitivity that flashes out a warning if a situation is brewing where we need to tread carefully. In this way we can transmute our capacity to feel shame into a healthy signal for us to slow down, witness ourselves and pay heed to those around us with clear communication.

Examples:

Joe's dad drove an old station wagon. Kids on the street would laugh at it as they drove by, making fun of the clunky old car. His whole family felt ashamed. Joe believed there was no escape from the family shame, he felt powerless. He internalized this feeling, which resulted in a loss of energy in his solar plexus area. Still today he feels that sense of powerlessness, deferring to others by habit.

Tom's mother caught him masturbating at the age of twelve. She yelled at him, calling him 'a disgusting animal'. Tom wished the ground could have swallowed him up. He swore never to pass this shame on to his children. Years later, his parents were visiting for a family party. Tom's four year old daughter started to masturbate herself in front of everyone. Tom's parents glared at him, then asked if he would stop her. Tom said no. He let her continue until her attention naturally shifted elsewhere. Later, he suggested to his daughter that when she feels like she wants to touch herself there she might prefer to find a private place where she wouldn't be disturbed. Her response was precious. She said, "Oh, like when I pick my nose!"

Celia's father criticized her nearly every time she opened her mouth. She grew ashamed of her expression and withdrew into isolation where her thoughts were her own. She felt judged for having needs and was unwilling to burden her father with her desires as they seemed to upset him. As an adult she continued that pattern of being 'seen but not heard'. She never spoke up for herself or had the courage to ask for what she wanted. Celia continued playing out this victim pattern until she became aware of its source. Now she is learning to find her voice and re-discover the empowerment of free expression.

Raymondo's Healing...

When I met Raymondo I noticed he was withdrawn and had a very soft voice. He admitted to me he had a trust issue and expressed a desire to heal it. We set an intention for guidance to help in this matter and I asked him to go back in time to when this issue originated. This is his story.

When he was seven years old, Raymondo's mother sent him and his two brothers to church choir. Each boy was asked to sing a solo. After Raymondo sang, the priest said, "We don't need you. You can leave." He returned home, feeling ashamed of his bad voice and sad that he was kicked out of a group he wanted to join. When he got home, his mother did not believe that he had been asked to leave the choir. She dragged him back down to the church and confronted the priest about it in front of all the other boys. The priest confirmed that indeed, Raymondo's voice had been so bad he was not going to be allowed to sing. Raymondo felt humiliated for a second time.

As a result of this incident Raymondo set up a belief that if he spoke his truth he would not be believed. This belief has cost him intimacy in relationships and led to him being withdrawn and aloof. He also believed that people did not like his voice. Hence his quiet voice and reluctance to speak. He felt rejected, too, like he didn't belong and had led a life of relative isolation as a result.

We set about healing these patterns and clearing the cellular memory. First we revisited the incident, and Raymondo felt the pain of the shame in his heart. We defined the afore-mentioned beliefs that had been set in place. Then we went back to the scene again and this time allowed Raymondo to speak his truth to his mother and the priest, telling them what he was feeling and what he really wanted. Once his inner child felt complete with this, Raymondo was able to integrate the part of himself that had split off that day back into his consciousness. Then, to reframe the old, painful memory, he imagined his ideal scenario taking place, of full acceptance in the choir and even being picked as a soloist!

He was angry with his mother for not believing him and had held a grudge against her. We explored the bigger picture of why this incident could have been helpful to make him who he is today. He realized that he had become independent and strong as a result of isolating himself. When he saw that, he could forgive his mother for the part she played in this. He felt warmly towards her again and the anger dissolved. He breathed that love back into his heart to heal the pain that had been stored there. He started to feel lighter and clearer, more relaxed.

I gave him two affirmations. One was, "My voice is perfect just the way it is," and "I speak my truth firmly without attachment to outcome." I also gave him the homework of speaking out more, expressing himself whenever possible, to lay a new groove down in his consciousness that it was now no longer shameful to share his feelings.

Exercises:

1. Write down all the times in your life when you have felt the shame of failure. See if there is a pattern. Work with the inner saboteur to heal this (see Chapter 1).

2. Make a list under two column headings: 1. Things I like about my body 2. Things I don't like.
    Then offer all these preferences up to Spirit for healing so you can come into loving acceptance of your body. Practice loving the entire list with equanimity.

3. If you have a partner or close friend, ask them to wash you in the bath or shower like a baby. Or wash each other's feet. Let yourself surrender to receiving this gift. Feel you deserve it!

4. Write down the sensitive issues of your sexual history, or share them with a friend. Did you ever feel sexually inadequate? Were you ever told you were a lousy kisser, had too small breasts or penis, or were not responsive enough? What happened to you as you heard that, or anything similar? Do you still believe it? Write or speak about any incidents that carry a charge for you. If appropriate, internally visualize giving back the criticism to the shadow side of the person who originally shamed you.

5. How did your family shame you? Journal about the times you remember being shamed by a parent, sibling, grandparent, or other relative. Write about any beliefs you created about life as a result. Internally visualize giving back the shaming words to the shadow side of the family member who shamed you.

10.
HOW CAN I RESOLVE MY GRIEF?

"Tears are the language of the heart." Osho

It was 1:30 a.m. when I got the call from my stepmother; a call I had been dreading since my father had his first heart attack seven years earlier. She didn't need to say a word. I knew he had left us.

I put the phone down and plunged into the deepest grief I had ever known. It felt surreal, as though I was dreaming. Yet every cell of my body registered my grief and immediate physical changes took place. My digestive system collapsed and I couldn't eat for days. My nervous system felt overloaded and I couldn't sleep, despite tremendous fatigue. All I could do was to feel the pain of my sweet Daddy's passing and to allow myself to cry it out.

Three days later I was back in England for a traditional British funeral. My Dad and I had always been extremely close and when he left his body it felt like a piece of me was ripped out and went with him. Maybe it did.

Allowing the grief...
The best thing we can do when grief arises is to allow ourselves to express the emotion fully in whatever way feels authentic for us. As with any release of emotion, breath and sound help to move it out of our body so crying is nature's way of facilitating this release. I let out my grief in the form of wails, tears and moans, along with sharing anecdotes and memories of sweet times spent together. Some people need alone time to be with their private pain and memories. Others prefer to process with friends. We must not suppress the grief, as suppressed grief morphs into unhealthy behaviors such as anger or bitterness that will rear their head at a later date.

I will never forget the national outpouring of grief over Princess Diana's death. England closed down for a week as British people everywhere honored the princess by taking time to cry and allow what had happened to sink in. Just as the tragedy of 9/11 opened hearts and elicited an unprecedented amount of prayer and energy worldwide, Diana's passing brought the British people together in a unified current of grief that bathed the nation in collective sorrow. Oh, how we felt for princes William and Harry as they stoically followed their mother's coffin to Westminster Abbey hardly shedding a tear. I only hope they were allowed their private time to grieve away from the eyes of the world.

So what did this do for the British public? It was as though the collective grief elevated us to a new level of love. People were kinder to each other, more loving and considerate. Neighbors spoke to each other, more old ladies were helped across the street, family members were appreciated and the precious gift of life was recognized by all. Hearts opened and love pierced the usual British armoring. Ironically it boosted us all. It was an expansive time, a raising of the collective vibration.

It didn't last. Like a drug that wears off, pretty soon peoples' behavior returned to the normal contracted state. But we didn't drop back down quite as far. There was a lingering after-effect that remained, and that may be the real gift Diana gave her nation.

Why we must grieve...

Grieving helps us to accept the loss that has happened. It is a catalyst for transformation, so we can process the change and release the past. Grief helps us to accept the situation and let go of what was, so we can be present with *what's so*. When we grieve fully we release the energy of sadness from our cells. Once the process feels complete and the emotional charge is gone, we feel lighter, free again.

There are two kinds of grief, our own personal grief over deaths, the end of relationships, hopes and dreams being dashed or eras ending. Then there is collective grief. This is the grief we share as humans, the misery of the ages, which is stored in our cellular memory. When we cry we can cry for everyone, not just ourselves. We can offer up our grief for healing the collective wound of sorrow that we carry as a species.

At the core of our grief is our sense of separation from God. Losses in this world trigger that original pain and remind us of that first sorrow we experienced as a soul. For me, ending relationships has triggered this pain of separation. It evokes the sense of being alone, cast-out and unloved. In moments of deep grief I have felt my anger towards God surface. It has been an opportunity to yell and scream and let out the stuck anger which has been wedged between me and my Divinity. Afterwards a deep peace has enveloped me and my sense of separation has lessened.

Rituals...

Taking time for rituals to mourn helps collect and solidify our grief. Cultures the world over have developed funeral rituals to bring together loved ones of the departed in order to say a final farewell, honor their blessed life and share in the grief. I was a wreck the day of my Dad's funeral. Yet that was appropriate! This is why we set aside time to perform these funeral rituals. I noticed that once it was over, the energy lightened up for me almost immediately. I felt 'all cried out' and complete with the fullness of my grieving time. I had devoted myself fully to the grieving period and after the funeral it felt done. Now I could move on to a new phase of life knowing that my Dad is always with me, he has just changed form.

We can use rituals to transform the pain of grief to the beauty of grief. Times of deep grief put us in an altered state, and we can bring forth expressions that are not normally accessible. We can express our grief through song, art, poetry or movement, creating something of beauty from our pain. This helps us move the energy of grief through our bodies in healthy ways. Maybe we draw our feelings in a work of abstract art, or we dance out our grief energy until we are exhausted. It doesn't matter if the expression is public or private. This is for us, a way to express our love for the one who's gone in a way that honors the relationship.

Elton John wrote the song, "Good-bye English Rose" for Princess Diana's funeral. I imagine that using his musical genius to create a song of such beauty was healing for him and all who heard that beautiful song.

The opportunity of grief...

Grief blasts through our armoring and melts our heart as effectively as deep love. Indeed, it is a mark of our love, a measure of the loss we feel when the object of our love is gone. It has the power to eat our ego by re-establishing perspective with life. Our normal personality crumbles in the flood of this deep emotion, leaving us soft, open and available. If there are family rifts, this is the opportunity for healing them. As the ego dissolves, past hurts and grievances disappear and we become open to a deeper, more connected relationship with those who are sharing this experience. Mountains of old judgments and resentments can be quickly moved through at this time. In our open, loving state we are more likely to forgive past betrayals, take responsibility for past actions or share a moment of gratitude for those close to us.

When my father died, despite my immense grief there was sweetness amidst the sadness. My four half-sisters and stepmother were brought together for the first time in years. Our shared grief melted our defenses and opened our hearts and I felt a closeness to all of them that had not been there before. We pledged to stay in touch, despite the obstacle of living in different countries. Now that we can no longer rely on Dad to bring us together we know we must do it ourselves. I felt huge gratitude to my sisters for their willingness to keep in touch with me, a far-away sibling they had hardly known. With my stepmother I had an opportunity to thank her for all she had done for me and for loving Dad for thirty-five years. It felt like a completion for me with her, a closing of a chapter of my life in the role of stepdaughter.

Once when I was grieving deeply I experienced a shattering. I fell apart, lay on the floor and wailed, becoming completely dysfunctional. Yet this was a very powerful time that opened me up in new and unexpected ways. When we are vulnerable and open like this we get reconfigured by our spirit guides. Our energetic system can be rewired, allowing us to vibrate at higher frequencies and experience deeper levels of love and compassion. In these moments of deep grief we are also more easily connected to God. It's God that picks us up and carries us in spirit arms when we are down. We rest in that changeless peace.

The cost of repressing grief...

In many countries working people are given three days bereavement leave. If we have lost a loved one this is rarely enough time to complete our grief process, yet society pressures us to go to the funeral and then miraculously return to work as normal. If we feel we are not given an opportunity to fully express our grief in a natural way and in our own timing we become resentful. This resentment gets buried inside us along with our unexpressed grief.

Suppressed grief leaks out in unhealthy ways. A part of us feels guilty that we have not fully grieved so we continue to mask it with numbing behaviors. Our relationships are less healthy, we hit the bottle or we shop till we drop. We get angry or irritated over small concerns and use the anger to cover up layers of sadness hidden deep inside. Then we go see a sad movie and the grief comes pouring out as we allow ourselves to be moved from within by the on-screen drama. If this is the case, there is still action we can take to complete our grieving process....

Grief for completion..

If we neglected to grieve a life-changing event at the time it happened, it's not too late to do it now. We can open up our 'grief case' and express the pain and sadness we are holding. We can call in the spirit of the person involved and speak to them as though they are here; we can write a letter addressed to them, that we don't have to send, or do the completion ritual outlined below. This is particularly important for healing past relationships, as any unresolved pain will remain as stuck energy in our cells and turn into resentment and complaint at a later date.

All of us were wounded as children. It's just a matter of how much. Some of us were severely abused, others had loving parents who just didn't know how to treat our fragile spirits. We weren't heard, our feelings weren't considered or we were disciplined in inappropriate ways. Whatever happened when we were young, there comes a time when we need to grieve the sorrows of our youth. We can write a letter to ourselves, starting with "I felt sad when….." and keep completing the sentence until we have expressed all of our hurts. Maybe we want to cry with the child we were or just embrace them tenderly in our hearts.

Another way to heal our wounded child is to ask a friend to sit with us and take turns talking to them as though they are our mother, father or other relative who wounded us. Our friend listens silently as we speak our deepest hurts, resentments and pain. When we are finished, our friend can hug us to comfort the little child that we were.

When we allow ourselves to grieve the ending of relationships or situations it helps us to feel complete with that part of our lives. If we don't do this there is a tendency for us to hang on to the past, remaining energetically attached to what was. Everything changes in our world. We move houses, jobs and cities. We lose pets, partners, friends and family. I have found that with each big change in my life it has been important for me to take some time and honor the person, place or thing I was moving away from.

Moving house has often been an emotional time for me. Houses contain beautiful memories of sweet time spent. Last time I moved I went from room to room thanking the room for hosting me and remembering particular experiences there. I felt sadness at leaving, yet having done this ritual, once I finally left the house I didn't miss it. I felt complete with my time there and accepted fully the change that was happening.

On our death-bed we grieve the loss of this life and all our disappointments. We don't have to wait until then to do this. We can take a look right now at the legacy we are leaving. What do we regret the most? Do we have dreams that we never had the chance to complete? Are we leaving behind beauty or chaos? It is a good exercise to imagine that we have six months to live and see what would be important to us in how we spent our precious time and energy. A life lived fully can be celebrated, with no need for regret and remorse.

Completion Ritual

We can take a quiet moment, close our eyes and revisit the person, place or thing we need to complete with. It can help our ritual if we light a candle and look at a photograph of what we are grieving. Then we take some deep breaths, allowing emotions to rise. We feel what energies are still in our bodies that want to come forth and be expressed now. Maybe we cry, rage or laugh or start to talk to the photograph about what we are feeling. Our tears honor the love we shared with that person, its depth and meaning for us. We do this until the energies are fully expressed.

If we are grieving a lost relationship it's important to cut energetic cords and cauterize their ends so we can be free of attachment as soon as possible.

We end with a thank you, to acknowledge the role this person, place or thing played in our lives.

Examples:

My friend Steven had a long-standing friendship and business partnership with his buddy Thomas. At some point relations began to sour. Some things happened that caused resentment and blame, yet neither of them were willing to confront the other about their deteriorating relationship and chose to hide from each other instead. Eventually Steven decided to leave the country and the business. The partnership with Thomas ended on a sour note. When I met Steven he was complaining of a pain on the left side of his chest. It started about the time he left Thomas and the business. I asked him how he felt about Thomas and what had transpired between them. Steven admitted his sadness, yet he had not told Thomas how bad he felt that he had lost him both as a business partner and as a friend. I suggested he spend some quiet time feeling this pain of loss, grieving it. Then I suggested he write to Thomas and tell him how sad he was. He did, and the pain in his chest went away.

Years ago when I sat with my jnana teacher, one of my fellow students, Mike, came in and announced he had lost his sixteen year old cat. Mike was very bonded with his cat and was feeling huge grief at the loss of his furry friend. Yet he was judging himself for these feelings. After all, as a respected lawyer he felt some shame around displaying such sadness in front of people who knew him professionally. My teacher was very clear. He said, "You honor your relationship with your cat with this grief. The sadness you feel is a mark of the love that you shared. Let it express itself."

My friend Tom has a brother, Mark, who is quite unlike him. Whilst Tom is a democratic, peace-loving vegetarian, his brother is an ex-military hunter who shuns company. As the younger brother, Tom always craved a deep and loving relationship with Mark, yet Mark was verbally abusive and mean to Tom and the two have been estranged for many years. Tom finally saw that he had closed his heart to his brother and this had affected his capacity for intimacy in other relationships. I advised him to grieve the relationship with his brother not being the way he wanted it to be. In this way Tom could open back up to a renewed capacity to get close to others.

Jeremy was twenty-one years old when he lost his best friend to a freak climbing accident. Jeremy grieved deeply, but amidst the grief realized there were gifts too in his friend's passing. His circle of friends bonded more deeply. He appreciated his own life more and felt his heart blasted wide open for the first time. Somehow Jeremy found an inner strength to move on with his life in a new, more connected way.

Exercises:
1. Grieve your inner child as above. "I felt sad when..."
2. Ask a friend to be a surrogate parent. Speak to them as though he/she is that parent, expressing all your hurts and resentments. The friend listens silently and hugs you when you are complete.
3. Go back over past relationships. Make a list of any unhealed wounds that are there and do not feel fully grieved. Write a letter to that person that you do not need to send.
4. Do the Namaskar yoga practice for letting go of grief. Using my "Floor Series" yoga DVD, add moaning and wailing to the movement. This is best done in a group.

DEATH VISUALIZATION

You just got a call from the doctor. You have one week to live. What is your reaction? Notice what closure you need with your affairs and with the people in your life. When were you disappointed with the cards life dealt you? What regrets do you have? What dreams did not manifest for you?

Now go to your death-bed scene. People have flown in from all over to be with you. See who is there. What are they saying to you? How are you feeling about your impending departure from this world? Do you have any last wishes?

Now see yourself breathing your last breath...what are your final words? Who do you speak them to?

Now you have died. There is no more 'I'. Your beliefs, ideas and personality are all gone. Poof! Feel what this is like. You see your body lying there and the grieving people all around it, yet the Essence that is you remains, observant and aware.

Suddenly you see an angel approaching. This angel tells you that you have been given a reprieve! You are being sent back to your body! But it will be different now. There is nothing left to fear. After all, you already died. You dropped your patterns and conditioning and they will remain absent, as long as you occupy this body. How does life look now? How will it be different? What is the first thing you will do?

Now fast forward through your life with this new awareness. See how this sense of liberation can permeate your new life. Breathe deeply into it. Be grateful for the freedom you now feel, as you are no longer bound by the mistress 'fear'. Feel the love that is present when the fear is gone.

11.
WHO'S GUILTY?

"When you feel guilty your ego is in command because only the ego can experience guilt."-Course in Miracles.

G reg had been abused by his father as a child. Beaten, shamed and criticized, his wounding ran deep. Not knowing another way to parent, Greg inflicted the same treatment onto his own son. The victim had become the tyrant. He felt guilty at this behavior and this guilt ate away at his self-esteem. He labeled himself a 'cruel parent' and felt that he deserved punishment for the abusive acts. Unable to forgive himself, Greg sabotaged his own life, creating a litany of money worries, relationship difficulties and back pain.

Guilt is an illusion. It is an egoic judgment that carries punishment—in our heads! Guilt is a rejection of the state where we find ourselves, a resistance and an unwillingness to accept ourselves fully as we are. It is not an emotion; it is a saboteur containing elements of self-judgment, fear, shame and anger. It is self-perpetuated, self-inflicted violence that deflects us from experiencing our original emotions by overlaying them with images and stories. Loving ourselves requires that we dive beneath the guilt to be with these deeper emotions so we may process them as necessary.

Guilt is often suppressed deep down in our unconscious. It has its origin in religion, what our parents told us, expectations placed upon us and our own behaviors that we judge as bad. We are taught that guilt calls for punishment and that this punishment will follow us even beyond the grave, so we persecute ourselves now hoping to lessen the punishment we believe is coming later. Self-punishing addictions such as alcoholism, drug abuse, work holism and perfectionism are all signs of suppressed guilt.

Original sin…
In western culture the program of original sin is still running our conditioning. The legend implies that when Eve ate the apple from the Tree of Good and Evil, mankind descended from the bliss of oneness into the pain of polarity and duality. The belief that there is a right and a wrong began and with

it our concept of sin. Our 'wrongdoer' has tormented us ever since. We judge ourselves as being wrong and worthless and call this the 'human condition'. This belief that we have 'sinned' is the underlying source of our guilt, which produces a corresponding fear that God will punish us for unworthiness.

Original sin is the idea that at our core we are bad and that our bodies are dirty. It is a deep-seated belief about the polarity of good and evil. Our religious and cultural conditioning around this runs deep and it can be challenging to wipe out these beliefs. Women, the descendants of Eve who tempted Man from the Garden of Eden, are seen as especially sinful. This feeling that we are intrinsically bad must be uprooted at the deepest, spiritual level. Many of us need help with this from therapists or spiritual counselors. We can also pray and invoke our guides and angels to assist us.

Hypnotherapy can be a useful technique for reprogramming such deep-seated beliefs. In a light trance state we can regress to the origin of the belief in original sin. Once we see that this belief was imposed upon us, it is easier to release. We can use deep breathing techniques to envelop feelings of guilt and unworthiness with love and acceptance. Plus, the more we learn to drop out of ego and into Presence, the easier it becomes to let go of all borrowed or imposed beliefs.

An investment in our own suffering....

Guilt is an abusive relationship with the self. When we feel guilty we feel unlovable, unworthy. We can't forgive ourselves, so we create self-sabotage, motivation for self-punishment and ultimately self-destruction. For example, we may manifest back problems or a lack of creative energy that stops us from doing anything praiseworthy. Or we set ourselves up for failure by saving money then blowing it all or losing it. In relationships we set up a barrier to intimacy that stops us from getting close to others because we feel unworthy of love. None of this is required behavior!

Holding onto guilt makes us feel like we are under attack. It justifies our anger toward ourselves or others and devastates our sense of peace and confidence, leaving us feeling fearful and empty. Look at what we blame ourselves for! 'Shoulds' are self guilt-tripping practices. They are often rooted in belief systems which are not true. For example, our beliefs about health. We 'should' exercise daily. We feel guilty when we don't and beat ourselves up about it. Blaming ourselves leads to depression and anger, leading to yet more guilt.

It's useful to discern if what we are telling ourselves we 'should' do is a *must*. We do this by dropping the shoulds into the heart and asking the heart if they are for our higher good, and if so, how we carry them out. If the heart's wisdom guides us in a certain direction we move forward with conviction, joy and passion. If the 'should' is not necessary we drop it.

With others....

One of ego's jobs is to keep us feeling separate by reinforcing feelings of fear and guilt. To survive, it encourages us to look for more guilt in ourselves and others, which in turn generates more fear and less love.

When our love for another person is conditional, we use guilt as a manipulation. We say, "If you love me you would do this/that" rather than accepting their authentic behavior. We blame others, acting from the victim consciousness mode of 'they did to me' rather than the higher place of 'it's all for me'. We make up stories to justify our guilt and the guilt of others. We try to get others to agree and support these stories.

Often when we condemn and criticize others we are projecting our own guilt onto them and reinforcing our own sense of unworthiness. For example, we see a drunk lying on the street and we judge him harshly. He is only reflecting to us a time when we acted irresponsibly and judged ourselves for it. His behavior is a call for love, to him and to us. If we can see him as whole and perfect despite his appearance and reflect that back to ourselves we can heal the suppressed guilt. Without the drunk and our awareness, our self-condemnation would remain intact and repressed. Life put him in our path to give us the opportunity to see our own self-judgment more clearly. Once we understand this, we can see any situation that triggers deep feelings as a game for our learning and understanding. We seek out places where the charge of condemnation lies and see it as an opportunity for our own healing.

Guilt vs. regret...

Guilt is based on morality and the idea of good and bad. Regret and remorse are about the choices we have made and wishing in hindsight we had made a choice that was more in alignment with our soul. If we have created pain for others by our negative choices and hurt them in some way, we own up to our flawed behaviors and become a better and stronger person from this awareness. Bringing our imperfect past out into the open helps us to be clear with ourselves. We can have no self-respect without fully feeling and owning our weaknesses. When we feel the pain of what our unloving behavior did to others we are released from it.

We can then have regret rather than guilt. We learn from our mistakes, admit we were less than conscious, then let them go. Confession (honesty) is good for the soul, the idea behind the Catholic confessional. It's not that we feel we have done something wrong, but instead recognize we could have made a higher choice and learned from the choice we *did* make. Then we can practice gratitude for our lessons instead of blaming ourselves and feeling guilty. We thank the other person for showing us something we needed to learn. We acknowledge and own our behavior and can also encourage the other person to examine any trigger that may have arisen for them. We can say we feel bad/regretful about our behavior and that we went unconscious. If any form of restitution is necessary, if the wrongs can be righted in some way, we take care of it. Then we can let go of even the regret and accept the perfection of all things. In this way we use our 'conscience' as a positive force for taking responsibility for our actions and for acting in a caring way with consideration for others..

To drop the guilt…

We are released from the poison of our guilt by absolute forgiveness, both of ourselves and others. No one is 100% trustworthy all the time. We are human and we all make mistakes. With forgiveness we drop the idea that what we did was a sin requiring punishment and instead see it as a mistake that needed correcting. We can certainly see how we may choose to act differently another time. We forgive ourselves by understanding we did the best we could at the time and move on.

Having said that, it can be a useful exercise in self-forgiveness to make a list of all the people we feel we have harmed by our actions. If we have done something we regret or feel bad about we can tell the truth about it to the people involved. The truth shall set us free from any burden of perceived guilt! If we know how to contact them, we can call them and 'make amends' by owning that we behaved unconsciously. Or we can do a silent prayer of self-forgiveness and call for a release from any energetic thread from our past actions that could bind us to these people.

Remember Greg? Years later, as Greg became more conscious of his behavior patterns and their source, he plucked up courage and talked to his adult son about his childhood. Greg apologized for the abuse, asking for forgiveness. His son was overcome with gratitude for this turn of events, forgiving his father and welcoming him back into his heart. Greg's life has also turned around. He has been able to drop the guilt and no longer sabotages his life.

Innocence...

The opposite of guilt is innocence. When we choose to see ourselves and others as innocent, we are able to expand into a more loving, open state. In addition, if we are authentic there is no room for guilt, as we are acting to our highest potential in any given moment and living our truth on an ongoing basis. Guilt and its sister, shame, drown in a sea of open, expansive love.

Examples:

One of my jnana group members, we'll call him Lance, is a mailman. One day, after seventeen years on the job, he did the unthinkable and forgot to deliver an Express Letter! This is a huge no-no in the Post Office world! Feeling guilty and ashamed of his error he returned to his depot and wrestled with how to handle his mistake. He noticed his desire to be the perfect employee and not get into trouble. He noticed he had fear of being fired and a motivation to somehow hide his forgetfulness. The guilt troubled him deeply. In the end he decided to simply go to his supervisor and come clean about it. The supervisor gave him a verbal warning and he was off the hook! He immediately felt relieved and absolved. The truth set him free from the guilt.

When I got divorced I had a mountain of credit card debt. I could have declared bankruptcy but it would have cost me money I didn't have, so I chose to do nothing and let the creditors call and harass me. I felt bad about this and assumed my guilt was because I had not paid my debts, which is against my regular character. But when I looked deeper I saw that I had not forgiven myself for the entire experience of being pulled out of integrity during my marriage, of allowing my husband to bully me into decisions that went against my better nature. It had not felt right at the time, but I was feeling too disempowered to do anything about it. I was attached to my marriage. Finally I embraced my younger self, told her I knew she did the best she could and merged her with me in love. Now I know I have cleared the guilt from that period of time. It no longer disturbs my peace.

My friend Louise gave herself a 'bad parent' guilt trip. Louise's daughter was diagnosed with scoliosis at the age of fifteen and was told that she potentially needed surgery to correct her spine and should come back for a check-up in three months. Louise heard the doctor but forgot to schedule the check-up. By the time she took her daughter back to see the doctor, seven months had passed and her daughter's spine had deteriorated so badly that she now needed major surgery. Ten years later the daughter still has back pain and Louise has carried with her the guilt of not being a responsible parent. After working with our jnana group on guilt, she decided to sit her daughter down and confess these feelings of guilt to her. She said she had not intended to neglect her, but she wanted to take full responsibility for her forgetfulness and also let go of the guilt. Her daughter listened intently and said, "Mom, you did your best and I forgave you long ago for this. Besides I don't feel like a victim here." Louise was relieved and also noticed that another blessing had come from this. It had sharpened her alertness for issues needing her attention in a timely manner!

Exercises:

1. Examine guilt as it comes up on a daily basis. Do an inventory every night. Check in with yourself and see if there is anything you can't forgive yourself for today. If you find you are holding onto guilty feelings, take time to journal about them and look for the lessons involved. Then drop the guilt feelings into your heart, transforming them into regret for the action taken, gratitude for the lessons learned and ultimately self-forgiveness and peace.

2. Write about events in your life when you feel you behaved badly. Be sure to describe all the ways you may have hurt other people involved. Write a letter of apology to each of them. It is not necessary to send this letter!

3. With a partner: Your partner is your confessor. Talk about your guilt. All the things you have not forgiven yourself for. Then spend some moments allowing the Divine to wash it all away with love. Run the guilt feelings out of your body down a silver grounding cord. Let your own Divine light run down through the top of the head, cleansing the places where the guilt had been hiding in the body.

12.
WHO'S THE VICTIM?

"I have sent you nothing but angels." Friendship with God, Neale Donald Walsch

In some part of each and every one of us lurks the archetype of the victim. We believe that life is unfair and that random circumstances are creating our suffering. Like most of our misery, the tendency to create the victim role comes from our wounds, past experiences and a sense of separation. When we feel separate we feel alone and fearful. We struggle in our lives and blame others when things go wrong. We become addicted to the familiarity of this suffering, which we mistakenly believe we are powerless to change and unconsciously draw into our lives circumstances that reinforce this belief.

Barry came on a yoga vacation with our group. I started noticing a pattern of complaint with him, when it appeared that he could never get what he wanted. The food was too spicy; he was given the wrong hotel room; the taxi drivers didn't understand him. He was constantly on the defensive, feeling like 'everyone was out to get him'. The point was driven home in a humorous way when we went snorkeling and one aggressive, hungry little fish (all of two inches long) bit Barry so much that he was forced to get out of the water! What was going on here? It became clear that Barry was playing the role of victim. When we addressed it, he admitted this was a life-long pattern. He confessed to getting pleasure from complaining and 'being right'. He was a man who was not at ease with himself.

Victim energy is a bit like a virus stored in certain files of our bio-computer, for example, the money file or the relationship file. In other parts of life we could be very successful, but if the victim virus is lurking in a particular file it will continually recreate suffering in that arena of life. This in turn creates a disturbance that affects our entire system. Fortunately, there are keys that unlock these patterns of victimhood. Activating our witness consciousness, identifying our tendency to play the victim role and shining the light of our awareness on our behavior are the first steps. Then we can take responsibility for ourselves and make new choices about our responses and our behavior.

Characteristics of a victim…

When we are in a victim identity we feel comfortable with our chosen role of sufferer. We perceive that we have been 'wronged' and revel in the attention it gives us. As victims we have given away our power and feel like we are not in charge of our lives. We feel vulnerable, scared and unsafe. We take no responsibility for our feelings and react to life's events in a melodramatic way, judging and blaming the players in our world. We identify ourselves as the helpless pawn being moved around by external events and in this state of denial, continue to attract similar circumstances to ourselves unless a shift into responsibility and awareness occurs.

As victims we complain a lot about our circumstances without speaking about how to shift them or taking action to change. Staying stuck in the complaint mode creates a downward spiral of negativity that sucks energy and can lead to depression. As victims we have a vested interest in our position. We feel glory in our martyrdom and gain sympathy and attention with our whining and complaining. It gives us permission to be angry, sad, to hold a grudge and remain stuck in the mire of self-pity. The world appears unfair and hostile. We feel helpless and are full of excuses as to why we cannot change our situation.

Why we maintain our victim story…

Some of us are addicted to our story. We repeat the same old grooves of victimhood in our own personal record of history and even go to multiple therapists and self-help programs for years without changing our patterns. As victims we describe life as a continuum of personal and professional disasters. We energize our wounded past and blame it for stealing opportunities from us that could have come our way. This is a story and an illusion, yet some of us derive great satisfaction in maintaining it because it gives us permission to lead a life of minimum expectation and limited responsibility. We get to lean on others for support and energy. We seek out people who are sympathetic to our story without challenging us to put it behind us. Since nothing is expected of the wounded personality we can never fail.

Our victim story becomes our language of intimacy with others. We bond with people through our wounds, exchanging tales of woe and self-righteousness. Giving up these stories can be painful because the story has become our identity. We are 'the one who was abused'. Through constant repetition of the story this victim identity is strengthened, which blocks our ability to transform and heal and keeps us stuck in our familiar, comfortable pattern.

The danger of defining ourselves by our wounds and refusing to let go of the past is that we lose our physical and spiritual energy and open ourselves to the risk of illness. If we are not working to get beyond our wounds, we stay stuck in the story about them and don't heal. In contrast, we can choose to learn from our experiences and gain strength and wisdom, plus the ability to be compassionate and tolerant. Usually we have learned much from our greatest hurts, often more than from times of fun and ease. If we are learning, can there really be a villain or a victim at all? No one has the power to make us feel a certain way. Someone's behaviors and words may elicit an emotion, but only we have the power to choose to stay stuck in our pain. The only person we can change is ourselves.

The extreme of suffering...

Let's play devil's advocate here and consider some extremes. My mother used to ask me, "What about the poor people who were tortured in the war in ghastly ways, weren't they victims?" I do have a response for her and for others curious about this question—the idea of the world being 'unfair'. So here I offer you a hypothesis—not a fact, just another perspective for your consideration, which you can either take or leave as you wish.

Imagine us as spirits before incarnating into this realm. We talk to our guardian angel about what experiences and lessons we choose to have in this upcoming life. Also we look at what actions from past incarnations can be worked out and balanced in this lifetime. We can call that karma (the universal law of cause and effect). Most of us have played the role of a tyrant at some time or other. As souls on the wheel of reincarnation we reap what we have sown, so it could be that in this upcoming lifetime the soul decides that it will balance its past actions by agreeing to play the role of a victim. This could include the experience of physical or emotional torture. A volunteer is found in the spirit realm who wishes to play the tyrant role for that soul. Contracts are drawn up and *whoosh*, the souls incarnate without remembering these agreements and the drama is played out.

Everything is for us, not against us.

Taking responsibility...

When we decide to choose responsibility for our life, a shift can happen. It's a movement back to remembering the purposeful nature of all things, and dropping the illusion of the small, separate self. As we grow in our spiritual path, we start to realize that our state of being creates our experience of life. We are the creators of circumstance, not its victims! If our internal state has attracted challenging circumstances, we can allow them and accept them in a flowing way rather than trying to resist them. We recognize our response is the only thing under our control and we choose calm instead of chaos. We blame no one for anything and instead are grateful to the players in our life-movie for their part in helping us get our lessons. When we take responsibility for ourselves in this way and add awareness to the equation, we lessen our suffering.

If we are a current victim of abuse, it would behoove us to ask why we have set our lives up to attract that situation. We can check and see if there is a pattern here. Maybe we made a decision in early childhood during a time when we were mistreated that made us believe that although this felt like unfair behavior, the adults must be right. This becomes a crucial choice point that locks in our beliefs about the world and will continue to attract situations that concur with that belief unless we can unravel it for ourselves. Children feel powerless over adults and develop behaviors and strategies for survival. However, these maintained childhood behaviors can create unhealthy dynamics when used in adulthood. As children we were not well equipped to respond differently. As adults we are. We can make new choices that empower and serve us today.

An advanced level of realization is to understand that everything in life is for our evolution, not against us. If we ask the question, "How can I benefit from this situation?" we can start to see how life encourages our growth, learning and compassion. For example, it could be that any abuse we endure is a motivator for our spiritual work, to kick-start our awakening process. We are in the depths of despair and think, "There must be more to life." So we start to look.

My friend Gail had her van stolen. Initially, she perceived it as a loss, that she was the victim of the theft. Then she got the gift, that it was a sign she was meant to move on and leave her current situation. She did move on and could eventually feel grateful for the theft.

Even pain can fuel this evolution if we know how to use it. We can learn to communicate with it, rather than taking the victim approach of thinking pain is bad and wrong and wanting to fix it. I know many people who have had life-threatening diseases yet have used the illness as a way to discover where healing was needed within them. Maybe they made poor choices for themselves and the pain is just a message from Spirit for them to choose again. Seen this way disease is a gift, not a burden. Physical illness may not always be cured but it can lead to a healing for us emotionally and spiritually if we so choose.

Adrienne was diagnosed with cancer. She decided to not tell those close to her, fearing they would be worried. She didn't want to be held in sympathy energy until she healed herself and got the lessons she needed from the disease. She took full responsibility for the cancer and set about investigating the purpose of the illness through hypnotherapy and natural healers. About a year after diagnosis, Adrienne had discovered so much about herself and had shifted so many old patterns and habits that she no longer cared about the cancer. It disappeared.

When people hurt us...

We may feel hurt by a person in some way but we have choices on how to respond. We can choose to feel victimized and attach meaning and story to the event, blaming and shaming others for our problems. Or we can choose the open, empowered, vulnerable path of the hero's journey and respond in nonviolent ways to our hurt, gaining strength in our defenselessness. This is the path of courageous gentleness despite provocation. No one can swerve us off our course of loving-kindness unless we choose. We may be abused, yet still feel compassion for the people who believe they need to be hurtful. We can set kind but firm boundaries for ourselves and others. "If you continue to speak to me this way I will hang up the phone/walk away." Then we must follow through to cement the boundary, which gives the other person an opportunity to look at their own way of being.

In this third dimensional realm of duality we can observe the spiritual law that all things turn into their opposites. Darkness turns into light, pleasure turns into pain. As victims we secretly covet the position of our tyrant and plot to overthrow them, to somehow turn the tables and take over the position of power. This means we have a tyrant inside of us. This whole victim/tyrant polarity needs to be healed so that we can come into a place of neutrality and balance where we wish only to be the equal of our tyrant. The most effective way to heal this is doing a square (see Chapter 7) where we can bring all of our unconscious thoughts out into the light of our awareness.

Our relationship with victims...

It is very important that we stay detached and do not identify with the suffering and victimhood of others, although we can feel compassion for their pain. If we hold them in the space of 'victim', we disempower them. A mutually empowering approach is for us to stay in our own truth and help them reframe their situation by encouraging them to take responsibility for what has occurred.

It is important to remember this if we have a tendency to be codependent and get value and self-esteem by 'rescuing' others who are in their victim mode. If we examine the pay-off we get for rescuing, we see how our behaviors are geared towards filling unconscious holes in our own psyche. The hook here is that by focusing attention on the problems of others we don't have to deal with our own!

Rescuing can interfere with peoples' choices and take away their lessons. It does not honor their God-self. When we can really honor the beauty of all their choices and not feel a need to jump in and fix them, the drama dissolves. Questions to ask ourselves that can serve as a guideline are: "Am I neglecting my own needs to resolve someone else's problem?" "Am I cheating this person out of an opportunity to solve a problem on their own?" "Am I enabling this person to continue being a victim?"

When we run across people who appear helpless such as starving children, beggars or abused women we must ask our compassionate heart as to the appropriate course of action, rather than the intellect and its 'shoulds'. If we decide to act and help, we can do so in a way that upholds their dignity and encourages and empowers them.

Examples:

Vicki was enmeshed in a victim dynamic with her alcoholic, abusive husband and demanding, disobedient children. She was controlling, trying to change their 'bad' behavior into 'good' behavior, which suited her own values. She dreamed of the 'perfect' family life. Her frustrations and failures resulted in resentfulness and anger toward them and herself. She became depressed and suffered from migraines and heart palpitations. One day she realized she needed help. She entered a CODA 12-step program and learned to be responsible for her own addictive tendencies. She realized she could only change her own behaviors. She started to set kind but firm boundaries for her family. Over time, changes occurred and new, healthier patterns became the norm. The physical effects of Vicki's codependent behavior disappeared and now she is emotionally healthy and happy.

My friend Stacy was always 'the one who was left out'. When she was a kid, she was the one picked last for teams, the one who was not invited to parties. Rejection was her theme. She felt victimized by others. She was left out because of 'their meanness'. Years later she was in an ashram in India where everyone was receiving 'prasad', a blessed offering of food. It was a cream puff. When she looked inside she found hers had no cream in it! Once again, Stacey had been left out! In the charged spiritual atmosphere of the ashram she suddenly came to a realization. She had created this theme of being left out! Her body didn't need the fat in the cream so she didn't get it! Her spirit was strong unto itself and enjoyed a lot of alone time. So it was perfect that she hadn't been socially accepted. Once she saw this her attitude around her theme changed and she felt she could embrace being rejected. Interestingly, after that she no longer got left out of anything!

My girlfriend was molested as a child. She chose not to tell her parents, but instead kept it all to herself; the shame, the guilt, and an idea that her parents could not be trusted to believe her. She held onto that story and suffered with it for forty-five years, continually recreating relationships where her belief that loved ones could not be trusted was played out. She experienced betrayal by friends and lovers time and again. Finally she told her parents about the molestation. They were supportive, yet sad that she had not told them at the time when they could have helped her. As a child she made the best choice she could, yet that choice kept her in victim mode and suffering for many years.

Exercises:

1. Discuss with a partner: What part of your bio-computer has the victim virus? How have you seen this manifested in your life? Pick one example and take responsibility for it instead, by discovering how it helped you learn or benefit.

2. Look more closely at a file that contains your victim virus. Write down all your beliefs associated with this file. For example, if it is money, it could be beliefs such as "I don't deserve to be rich" or "Only hard work will make me wealthy" or "I am not smart enough to make money or go to school."

    Find where these beliefs originated. Look at them from the perspective of the witness and see them for the illusion that they are.

    Write about the circumstances you have attracted that substantiate these beliefs.

3. Examine the payoff for staying in an unhealthy relationship. If this is a pattern, do exercise 2 for relationships.

4. Examine your tendency to rescue, acting out the codependent self. What is the payoff for you? What do you think you gain from upholding other peoples' stories, e.g. connection, empowerment, belonging, approval, identity, being busy and involved?

5. Do the square for 'Desire to be a victim/tyrant; fear of being a victim/ tyrant'.

CULTIVATING AWARENESS

Cultivating awareness involves learning to spot our old habits and patterns, and consciously choosing to act differently. We let go of our habit of making assumptions, release the need to make ourselves special, and make choices that expand us in new ways.

We commit to raising our vibration by having more fun in our lives, celebrating our time on the planet as creatively as we can. We feel more alive, spontaneous and able to live in our maximum potential in each moment.

13.
WHAT'S THE ASSUMPTION?

Some great all-time assumptions:
Man will never walk on the moon.
The Titanic can't sink.
Saddam Hussein has weapons of mass destruction.
Hitler will never amount to anything.
Man will never run a mile in under four minutes.
We are separate, finite beings.

One year I was leading a group retreat to Hawaii and had arranged to meet some of the students at the Kona airport. I assumed their flight details were the same as mine, as I had come in a day earlier on the same flight, so I did not ask them for their arrival details. It turned out I was wrong! They arrived earlier and at a different terminal! It was only by chance another group member saw them waiting and we connected. My assumption had nearly landed me in trouble!

It is our habit to make assumptions. The human mind has a need to understand, explain, rationalize and justify. Our emotional side likes to feel safe. Therefore the mind makes assumptions about anything it can't explain, even if the assumption is far from the truth. How often do we say, "Oh, but I thought….," only to stand corrected? We prefer to live in a fantasy world of illusion because we lack the courage to ask for clarity and risk getting an answer we may not want. We are afraid of what we don't understand. We are too scared or lazy to find out the truth, so it's easier to make an assumption.

The world is filtered through the veil of our perceptions that are personal to us. We 'make-up' stories, fantasies form, and we get caught up in them. Imaginations run wild and our minds spin needlessly out of control! We fit assumptions neatly into our belief systems. We believe something is the real truth, and then go even a step further and react to this fantasy truth. This can get us into even more trouble! We create misinterpretations, false expectations and misunderstandings, which in turn lead to disappointment and suffering.

Jumping to conclusions...

We must learn to discern between *what's so* and what the mind makes up about *what is so*. For example, we move towards our friend to give them a hug goodbye and they back away. We jump to the conclusion that they are angry with us. We could choose to hold onto that painful belief, which could well be wrong, or we could ask them why they don't want to hug, and find out the truth. Maybe they had a cold and didn't want to pass it on.

We must cultivate our witness enough to respond to what actually happened rather than our ego's interpretation of what happened. Otherwise we are not fully experiencing life as it is. If we catch ourselves wanting to interpret, we can own it by using the words "I imagine..." In the above example, we would clear up doubt by saying, "I'm imagining you don't want to hug me because you're angry with me." Then we wait for the response. Voicing our imagined assumptions is a great tool for keeping us real and for enhancing intimacy with our friends. It brings richness to our relationships that deepens with time and practice.

Judgment is another common jump to a conclusion. We assume we know what is good and bad and right and wrong. Yet we really don't. Everything that happens in the world is neutral. It's the meanings we attach to situations that give them a charge in our personal life-drama. The meanings are assumptions. The more we practice stepping back and observing from the witnessing position rather than energizing our mind's interpretations of what we see, the deeper we drop into peace.

Futurizing...

Our culture trains us to be over-concerned with the future, to the detriment of staying in the present. We are encouraged to 'save for retirement' and 'work hard today for a better tomorrow'. It's our habit to make assumptions about what is going to happen in the future and we get needlessly upset about our speculative fantasies. This is the antithesis of staying in *what's so*. It takes us out of the present and can be emotionally draining and unnecessary. It's also commonly known as worry!

When I was much younger I used to waste all kinds of mental energy worrying about what it would be like if I ever got married abroad. I worried that my dad would not be available to travel far away to come and marry me off. I assumed I would have no friends there, as they would all be back in England. It would be a miserable event attended by a meager few. As fate would have it, I met an American and did get married abroad. But the universe supported the wedding with amazing confirmations of synchronicity! My step-mother and children were booked on a ski trip that week leaving my dad available to fly to California and be with me for a whole week. New friends I had met in the States came to Tahoe for the wedding and it was a fabulous day in so many ways that I could never have imagined in my youth.

In relationships...

We assume others see the world as we do, through the same filter. We project our values and experiences onto them and assume we know what they need and what's 'good' for them. We don't! We are just making up stories about how we think it feels to be in their shoes.

Most people I know lead busy lives. They look at my schedule and project that I am busy, too. As a result they are often hesitant to call me for a lunch or dinner date. When we worked with assumptions in jnana group this came up as a myth I quickly dispelled! I have plenty of time for meals with friends as I make that a priority in my life.

We care-take people according to our assumptions about them. This is an egotistical practice that robs them of their own power. We tend to do it with our children in particular, projecting our own tendencies onto them. For example, my mother would insist I buy 'sensible' shoes when I was young, rather than the high heels I really wanted. She assumed I would rather be comfortable than glamorous. Once I got older and bought high heels, I realized her wisdom, but I needed to make my own decisions and sometimes I would still choose beauty over comfort!

We express love to our partners the way we like to receive love. It may not be their way, in which case they can feel unloved by us. We cannot assume we know what makes anyone feel loved. If we have not asked the simple question, "What makes you feel loved?" then we are guessing.

Bill feels loved by hearing that he is appreciated. His wife, Donna, feels loved by being touched. Bill appreciates her but is not much of a toucher and she touches Bill a lot but fails to verbally give him appreciation. Both partners feel dissatisfied with the relationship.

It's our responsibility to be as clear as possible with everyone in our lives so they don't have to make assumptions about us. If we withhold information there is less intimacy, less trust. When we are not transparent to our friends and partners, the tendency is for them to assume they know what we are thinking and feeling and that becomes their fantasy. People are not mind-readers. Yet if they don't do what we want them to do we feel hurt! All we need to do is to state clearly where we are at and what our needs are and all assumptions are dissolved.

Terry assumed that when she felt depressed her beloved didn't want to be near her. But when she asked him, she found out he enjoyed feeling useful by loving and supporting her at such times. She did not have to wear the mask of happiness to be lovable. Her partner appreciated being able to love her in her depressed state too, as it felt very real to him and he appreciated her vulnerability.

With ourselves...

Our most primary assumption is that we are separate, finite beings; that there is a 'me'. This limited belief invites states of loneliness, despair and lack, as our 'me' cuts itself off from the rest of existence, defining its boundaries with the body. If we take a moment to investigate where this 'me' is within us, something very interesting happens. When we really look, we can't find the 'me'! There are feelings, sensations and thoughts, but who is experiencing them?

The very question "Who am I?" helps us to drop into a state of expansive stillness, where mind chatter stops. Our assumed boundaries dissolve and we cannot find where we begin or end. This discovery is freedom! (More on this in Chapter 20.)

On another level, we tell ourselves stories about our own abilities. We think we can't do certain things. We over or underestimate ourselves. We deceive ourselves about who we are and what we really want. We even lie to ourselves to make ourselves right. The universe responds to these strong beliefs by reflecting back to us situations which seem to justify the assumptions. If we are not careful, we can be caught in a dangerous loop of thought and creation.

A common theme is the assumption about what makes us happy. "I will only feel fulfilled in life if I have a relationship/expensive car/nice house/good job." How do we know this is really true? Many times I have seen people lose jobs or relationships and discover that in fact they were better off without them! When we hold too many assumptions about ourselves we limit our possibilities in life and box ourselves up in a pattern of repeating our known experiences.

My friend Todd had a steady job with a secure income. He was a DJ at night and wished for more time to pursue this hobby, but always assumed he could not make it financially in the competitive world of the music business. His company down-sized and he lost his job. Suddenly he had plenty of time for music and started to put together his own CD's. Now he is a top DJ in our area and supports himself with music. He has never been happier.

How to stop making assumptions...

Correcting our tendency to make assumptions brings us from a fantasy world into a real world. We stop making assumptions about people by the simple act of asking questions! If we want to know something about someone, we should not ask a third party; that's how rumors and gossip start. We go to the source! We ask for clarity, clear communication and transparency from all those around us. When we question deeply it helps our friends become authentic and encourages them to communicate clearly. There are fewer misunderstandings in our relationships and we feel clean in our dealings with everyone around us.

I traveled to Thailand with my friend, Nikki, who is a highly conscious person and a delight to be with. On a daily basis she would share her inner dialogue with me about her assumptions. She might say, "I'm imagining that you are finding me boring or uninspiring as a companion." This would give me a chance to dispel her imaginings, clearing a space for us to travel smoothly together, with no mental 'stuff' impeding our relationship.

If we notice we are moving into fantasy, we stay with *what's so* and stop projecting into the future. We use our witness to see when our minds are going off in a future tangent and are vigilant at pulling our attention back to the present moment. We are content to let life unfold, resting in the unknown, allowing the mystery of it all to be revealed moment by moment.

Positive assumptions...

What if we had enough faith to assume that all life was for us, not against us? Faith can be a healthy assumption. We can assume that all is well, and trust that God is taking care of us.

There's a lovely story about a lady called simply Peace Pilgrim who wandered across America with nothing but a toothbrush. One night it was raining heavily and she was alone on a country road. She came across a bridge and underneath it she found blankets and a pillow! She trusted totally that God would always take care of her and created this reality on a continual basis with this assumption.

Rick is the manager of a hotel. He used to go to sales meetings assuming his staff was not prepared and that he had to do all the work. One week in jnana group we were all looking at our negative assumptions. Rick decided to shift his belief around his staff's capabilities into a positive assumption instead, to see what would happen. He allowed them to give input and lo and behold, a great plan was conceived, better than he could have done alone! It was less stressful, easier for him, and it empowered his staff.

Assumptions v. Intuition

Assumptions have qualities of judgment and logic. They come from the head. Intuition has qualities of a deeper, non-logical gut feeling. With both we need clarity, so we must still communicate and confirm our inner thoughts, no matter their source. Sometimes intuition can say one thing to us and our assumptions can negate that feeling. For example, my friend had an intuitive feeling that her husband was cheating on her. But her logical assumption was that he was not. It turned out her intuition was right.

Questioning our assumptions invites us into a place of innocence, a state of 'not knowing'. In the place of the unknown we stay open to all possibilities. No longer restricted by the box of our assuming mind, we are free to delight in the unlimited surprises of our unfolding life.

Examples:

When I was a teenager my dad always offered me wine with Sunday lunch each week and I always refused. Then when I turned fifteen, I went wine-tasting on a school trip to Germany and developed a taste for wine. I came home and the next Sunday shocked my dad by accepting his offer of wine! The point here is that my dad honored me by never assuming I would say no, even though he asked me the same question each week.

Cathy went to meet a new massage therapist and he did not show up. She waited and waited and began to notice she was making assumptions in her head about being stood up. Then she said, "No, I am not going there—something may have come up that I don't know about." She drove home feeling at peace and not angry or troubled. She later found out that she had been stood up, but at least she didn't drop herself into negativity at the time.

Sandy's boyfriend had gone on a business trip. He had given her his new pager number so she could reach him. She called and called and got no response. She got really worried, then angry, then sad. Her mind was spinning cartwheels with all kinds of assumptions as to what he was doing and why he was not returning her calls. It turned out he had simply given her the wrong pager number!

Exercises:

1. Write about the assumptions you make about yourself. 'I am this kind of person'. 'I can/can't do this/that'. 'I assume people think xyz about me.....' 'I can only be happy if....' Is any of this really true?
2. Watch your assumptions about people. Practice asking for more clarity.

3. In a group of three: Be brave—share your inner dialogue and tell the two other people assumptions you made about them—then get them to respond with the truth! Don't be nice. Notice if you take these assumptions personally!

14.
WHAT'S THE PATTERN?

When I first started running retreat weekends I was over-controlling, bossy and attached to a fixed picture I had in my head of how I thought everything should look. I micro-managed every little aspect of a retreat from the food to the planned-out content of classes so that everything would go smoothly and be as perfect as possible. I tried to control my students and would get upset if they wanted to deviate from my class structure. Of course, this didn't work very well. My students sensed my stress when things did not go according to my plan and I created an atmosphere of tension with my controlling attitude.

Luckily for me and my students I started looking at my patterns when I began studying jnana yoga and soon realized that I often behaved as a controller. It came from a belief that if I was in control, everything would turn out perfectly and then everyone would love me. I soon discovered that the opposite was true. To my astonishment I found that students liked it better when I was relaxed during an event and they could feel free to be themselves without fear of my judgment!

When I looked deeper at this pattern I found a scared inner child desperately holding onto the reins of control as a way to help her feel safe in the world. This, together with the desire to be perfect to gain approval and attention had led to a place where my whole world was formulaic and calculated, with little room for spontaneity and growth. It took many years of conscious work to break those ingrained behavior patterns. I discovered the value in being organized and prepared, yet flexible and spontaneous. Now I no longer even plan classes. They evolve organically from the needs of the students who show up.

Origin of patterns…

Most limiting beliefs that are the basis for our patterns are set up in childhood. As children we learn behaviors that allow us to survive and thrive in our family. We assume the role of the good little boy or girl, the clown, or the cute one. These are all manipulations and strategies that prevent us from being our authentic selves. After a while these patterns become automatic and ingrained. As adults we continue to magnetize to us people and events that correspond to our patterns, our inner pictures of how to survive. We perceive that our erroneous ideas about life are true.

Michele remembers her mother ignoring her constant childhood questions. The only way she could get her attention was to play cute or create a problem. Her real desire was to be treated with respect and to have connection with her mother. To this day, it is easy for Michele to slip back into the pattern of playing cute and telling jokes if she wants to connect with people. Now she is aware enough to witness when she is playing out that old behavior and to stop it, asking instead for the intimacy she truly desires.

Sometimes we create patterns based on our parents' beliefs. Our mother believes that she is a victim, so we do too. We learn to complain and believe that the world is against us because that is all we ever saw at home while we were young. Or the opposite can happen. Our inner rebel steps forward and whatever our parents' patterns were, ours are the opposite! Dad was an over-achieving, go-getter so we are lazy, aimless and laid-back. We must recognize all of our patterns and beliefs to see if they are still appropriate for us today.

Why we maintain our patterns...

As demonstrated in the movie, "What the Bleep?" the more we believe a thought, the more we activate an addictive emotional pattern. We feed and strengthen the pattern by repeating it until the tiny neural pathway becomes a super-highway! These patterns become familiar and feel comfortable. Even though they may not be logical, old patterns can still dominate our thinking today. They color our existence and take us out of Presence.

However, our unconscious mind may continue to recreate patterns because we have not yet completed the learning experience that they offer. The light bulb has not yet flashed on, so we must keep asking Spirit to help us get the lesson! For example, if we come from families, like I do, where everybody played nice and conflict was generally avoided, we must learn to acknowledge conflict before we can transform it. Instead of retreating and avoiding, we stand up for ourselves and speak out. Only then will a pattern of attracting conflict situations end.

How to determine our patterns...

Our patterns are based on our early childhood beliefs and programming, which make up the content of our stories. The stories we tell ourselves in turn create our lives, so looking at our personal history is a way to unravel our patterns.

To examine this further we can write out our sad story, 'The story of my life so far'. If we had to write a letter of complaint to God, this could be it! What are we sick and tired of? We may complain that we are always the responsible one that never has any fun, or we are lonely and isolated, or alienated, unsupported and misunderstood. When we look at our story we can find the energetic structure being held within our beliefs and see more clearly our patterns and programs. For example, if we were to write out our victim story we would see words of suffering, blame, specialness, powerlessness or worthlessness, entitlement and betrayal.

The first method to start clearing ourselves of these beliefs is to write down any charged words from our story in a column, and write out their opposites next to them. For example, blame/forgive; pain/pleasure. When we look at our list we see clearly the nature of duality, that there are opposing energies at work in the world. When this is complete we can pray for balance and offer our unhealed minds to Spirit for transformation. This is a simple way to bring ourselves into a place of neutrality, harmonizing the polar opposites of our minds.

The next step is to find the general theme of complaint. It could be abandonment (people leave me), fear (I play safe and stay stuck), anxiety (I'm always stressed and tense), anger (people irritate me) or victim (they did it to me). Then we can ask Spirit to take us back to where this pattern originated. We ask for memories to be shown us, to find our frozen inner child, the part of us that got split off from our authentic Selves, when this pattern and belief were established. We can ask how old we were. We let the child express emotions and converse with that child until we sense that our child is reintegrated within us.

Ed has a pattern of not allowing himself to have joy in his life. He is the hard worker, the responsible one. When he wrote his letter to God, his main complaint was that he didn't have any fun. On tracing this back he discovered a sickly child of three whose mother forbade him to go swimming or play outside with his friends in case he caught a cold. He saw then that he carried the belief that it was not OK for him to have joy. His mother's concerns echoed in his mind unconsciously and he would turn down offers of fun. Now that he sees the connection to his past and the illusion of the belief, it no longer has a hold on him. He is beginning to have fun in his life again!

Once we shine the light of our awareness on the distorted workings of our minds, our beliefs no longer have the power to run our lives. Everything changes. However we must continue to use our witness to see our old behaviors when they arise and continue to make new, healthier choices.

It may seem like there is a void, an emptiness, as our old ways are discarded and the new is not yet in place. This can feel like a vulnerable time, as we are literally re-wiring our brains. We must have faith in the process and allow it to unfold. When we empty ourselves of distorted thought patterns, the wisdom and love that are always within us can rise to the forefront. Our lives become juicy, spontaneous and joyful.

Clearing the pattern with inquiry...

The great advantage of proactively clearing our patterns is that the universe does not need to send us catastrophes to wake us out of them! Our lives become smoother, less dramatic.

What follows is a line of questioning for self-inquiry into an erroneous belief or behavior that is messing up our lives. It can look something like this:

Friend: So Julia, do you have a behavior pattern you would like to look at today?

Julia: Well, I have a few. But for today I'd like to focus on my anxiety pattern that seems to come up when I get stressed and feel I have too much to do.

Friend: What is the benefit of having this anxiety?

Julia: Well, it spurs me on to get the things done that I need to do. It keeps me focused.

Friend: And if you get these tasks done what value is that to you?

Julia: Then I can feel relaxed and peaceful as I know I have taken care of business.

Friend: Does it help you to be anxious?

Julia: No.

Friend: Can you have this feeling of relaxation and peace without the anxiety?

Julia: Yes.

Friend: So is it true that you need to feel anxious in order to create peace and relaxation?

Julia: No.

Friend: Where did you first learn this pattern?

Julia: In school when I had lots of homework

Friend: What would your life be like without this belief?

Julia: More relaxed!

Friend: So now take some deep breaths and as you exhale say, "I release the belief that I have to be anxious in order to feel relaxed. I am relaxed and at peace."

Steps for Pattern Clearing:

1. Discuss your pattern or issue.

2. How does it make you feel?
3. How do you want to feel?
4. Is it familiar? Where did you first learn this?
5. Breathe into the issue. Allow it to be there.
6. What is the benefit of this feeling? The pay-off? Why am I invested in maintaining this pattern?
7. And what is the benefit of that? And the benefit of that, etc. Keep dropping deeper within until a positive core feeling is reached, e.g. safety, feeling loved, alive, peaceful, energized.
8. From this line of questioning we can draw a conclusion. In order to feel this core feeling I have to feel/ do……. (the initial behavior/ feeling).

    E.g., In the example given, I thought that in order to have peace, I first had to feel anxious.
9. Is it true?
10. What would life be like for you if you could let go of this pattern?
11. Does anyone benefit from you upholding this belief?
12. Breathe deeply and say, " I release my belief that…." Take it inside mentally and affirm this three times. If the inner child was involved with the creation of this belief, talk to the inner child so it too can release this belief.
13. Mentally affirm "I can now have this desired feeling of love/safety/ peace etc. whenever I wish."

In relationship…

Intimate relationships are great because they offer us the opportunity to see our unconscious patterns! If we do not examine these patterns our relationships become stagnant and rigid. One day the light-bulb goes on and we see that we are repeating the same old dysfunctional patterns in relationship after relationship. This is good! We are becoming conscious! Now there is a good chance the underlying patterns can be brought into awareness and healed.

Unless we have healed our relationship with our parents and cleared our childhood wounding, we will try to reproduce the family situation as adults in order to heal it! Oh shock and horror when we realize that we have played out the dysfunctional patterns of our parents or the family dynamic in our own relationships! We often 'marry our parents' so to speak, to enable us to replay and heal what was not healed before in their relationship or in our relationship with them. Or we gravitate to the polar opposite of our parents as an act of rebellion, acting out our anger. We then try to get from our partner what we missed receiving from our parents. It is vitally important that we see this! If not we will stay bound to our past, locked into a 'tragedy', a war that cannot be won.

When we looked at this in group one of my students realized he had been married for thirty years to the polar opposite of his mother. His mother had no boundaries, which he craved as a child. His wife was full of them! They had been miserable together for years but unable to break the ties and move on. After this realization my student felt cleared from this unconscious pattern and he and his wife were able to separate in a loving way.

My parents rarely revealed any confrontation. Growing up, I have no memory of witnessing anger or open, intimate discussions, so in relationships I did as they did. I hid my feelings and grew resentful and angry. It took a lot of courage, will and awareness to overcome that conditioning and confront issues as they arose. My pattern in relationship has been to withhold and withdraw. Too afraid of losing love, I tend to hide my authentic Self and retreat to my own inner world at the first sign of conflict. Now that I am aware of that pattern, I commit to being transparent in relationships and speak my truth regularly, clearly and without apology.

We also either adopt or reject our parents' attitudes towards the opposite sex. My friend Dana's father had nothing but constant power struggles with his wives. She learned that same pattern and has been in constant conflict with her male partners. My mother has the attitude that all men are bastards. So I rebelled and unconsciously adopted the attitude of 'all men are angels'. This led me to make excuses for men I was with, not seeing their faults clearly and generally being in denial about the real state of the relationship. I have had to let go of that in order to be real with myself and any man in my life.

Common relationship patterns:
'I'm not worthy'. Watch the saboteur mess things up here! People choose drama over serenity.

'I'm angry and hurt from past events and I am going to take it out on you, the one who loves me. I will break agreements in a passive-aggressive way to hurt you'.

'I'll lose your love, so I must withdraw without communicating what is wrong'.

'Codependence', where people stay hooked into unconscious patterns where true desires are subordinated to take care of someone else. The pattern here is an addiction to manipulation and approval.

'Withdrawal', where conflict is avoided at all costs and truth is hidden. No authentic communication takes place.

Habit patterns...

Like hamsters on a wheel, most of us are running our lives in a loop of routine. We get up at the same time each day, eat the same breakfast, drive the same route to work. We all have a tendency to get stuck in a comfort zone of what is familiar. We have mastered a set of behaviors and do not risk failure by abandoning these known patterns. Yet if we are to be truly free we need to create space in our lives for spontaneity and newness. Then every moment can be fresh and alive, without the drudgery of patterns and routines to draw us into the slavery of meaningless action.

Habituated patterns are a big trap. Any routine forms a rigid structure, which creates a veil around our consciousness, blocking us from seeing clearly. We become dulled and bored with life. Something in us switches off when automatic pilot is on. We lack inspiration and energy and stay stuck in our ways, resisting change of any kind. Our life force dwindles and we age more quickly. We create a mold for ourselves and stick in it like Jell-O. It becomes easier to believe the stories we tell about ourselves than to break free from them.

It's a great practice to spend a day behaving differently than normal. If we usually get up, make coffee and put on the TV before work, we could try taking a walk and having tea instead. I like to ask my body what it wants rather than moving automatically through my day and letting habit dictate my emotions.

Rick used to listen to the news on the radio each morning as he drove to work. He noticed it made him tense. He decided to change this routine and started playing a tape of positive affirmations instead. Now he arrives at work relaxed and in a positive state of mind.

Breaking out of the mold...

Conformity feels safe. We don't stand out in a crowd and can fade comfortably into anonymous oblivion without drawing attention to ourselves. Yet what if we march to the beat of a different drum? What if being stuffed into society's box of an education system and 9-to-5 work-place feels discordant with our being? Here is where courage is needed to be the rebel and dare to be different, even if it means confronting what is socially acceptable to everyone else.

Rosa Parks refused to sit down in the black section of the bus. Her one brave action started a revolution. In show-business, Madonna has consistently played the edge of what is considered socially acceptable on television and in books. The queen of reinvention, her unbridled creativity and willingness to push the limit have helped us all question our values.

When we let go of our need to stay in comfortable routines, habits and social conformities, we become more available to be fully present and alive in the moment. Spontaneous behavior happens, as we no longer block the invited flow of our lives. We get to expand the Creation with our own unique gifts.

Examples:
As an eight-year old boy with dyslexia my friend John was told by a neighbor that 'he would never amount to much'. He never forgot those stinging words and set out to prove her wrong. He became a hard-working entrepreneur and owned a company with three hundred employees taking in millions of dollars a year by the time I met him. Yet the overachiever pattern had turned into an addiction. He could not allow himself to fail and drove himself ruthlessly, despite poor health.

My student Jen had a pattern of being sick and depressed. When we inquired deeper and did the line of questioning outlined earlier in the chapter, she said she got weak and sick because it gave her attention. Her family pampered her. She felt loved. That left her feeling alive and energized. When she looked to see when this pattern first arose, she remembered being very hyperactive as a child and full of energy. Yet her parents couldn't handle her energy level and would put her down and criticize her. At five years old she got sick with pneumonia. Her parents showered love and affection on her. She felt better. At seven she had a car accident. Once again family affection was poured upon her. She formed a belief that said, "I have to calm down. People love me when I am weak or sick." So her conditioned neural pathway was to gain love and attention by getting sick. Once she saw that, she was able to release this addiction and find new, healthy ways to share loving energy.

Jim had low self-esteem his whole life, sabotaging himself financially and choosing unfulfilling relationships. When we did the exercise where he got to write to God and complain, he discovered his theme was 'not getting what he wants'. On tracing back the origin of this theme, he found his frozen inner child at around five years old waiting for his father. Jim's father would get drunk and forget to pick him up from school. Jim internalized this act as meaning he was not worthy of his father's attention and love. He saw clearly how that belief had held him down, creating patterns of mediocrity and failure where the belief could be substantiated.

Exercises:

1. With a partner: Pretend your partner is God. Tell him/her your sad life story with all its complaints! Then ask your partner to reflect back to you your main theme of complaint. Process it as explained in the chapter. Then switch roles.

2. With a partner: Use the line of self-inquiry questioning in the chapter to create new neural pathways for old beliefs and patterns. Then switch roles.

3. Write about your parents' relationship patterns. What did you learn from them? How has this affected your own relationship choices?

4. Examine habits and start to change them. For one day at a time, practice checking in with your body about what it wants rather than going by routine.

15.
WHAT'S SPECIAL?

The guru is like a flashlight—he shines light onto the path. Don't make the flashlight special!

My ego loves to make me special. It tries to convince me to feel superior, telling me I am better than others around me. These insidious thought patterns create a sense of separation between me and everyone else. Plus I've noticed that the other side of this polarity, my sense of worthlessness, is never far behind, ready to convince me that the opposite is true too. I am not good enough, not lovable, and can never get anything right. Special/worthless, superior/inferior; most of us swing wildly from one to the other as our ego tries to carve out our place in the pecking order of this world.

The fear of feeling worthless is counteracted by the ego's desire to be special, causing us to crave attention and approval. This prideful attitude leads us to identify with the idealized image we have of ourselves rather than our real, flawed self. It fosters the idea of 'becoming someone', the basis for ambitions of fame and worldly success. Specialness has inherent within it a feeling of separateness and judgment. We constantly compare ourselves to others to make sure we are getting 'somewhere'. This comparison addiction in turn fires up the polarity swing from superior to inferior and so can give us only temporary satisfaction.

Equality...
The concept of superiority is a very seductive idea. It has led us to justify crusades, wars and atrocities, causing untold suffering, because we have held the idea that we are right and 'they' are wrong. It creates separation. Ideas about superior nations, philosophies or religion divide us even further. We must deconstruct these erroneous belief systems by following these ideas back to their origins within us.

For millennia, patriarchy has led to men being held in higher regard than women. Indeed, our original sin programming perpetrates the blaming of the female for the evils of the world. This story has become an underpinning of the structure of consciousness, deeply embedded in our belief systems. We don the filter of this illusion like glasses, and it assumes a reality, as though we have stepped onto the 'holideck' of Star Trek. To balance our world we must embody equality between men and women and between all races. Then we can honor our diversity, yet see the equality we share as humans, all carrying the spark of the Divine within.

As we awaken, we begin to perceive with more equanimity. We start to see the world the way that Jesus did. From the glamorous Hollywood actress to the Indian streetsweeper, as we accept all people fully for the roles they play in the world, we ourselves come into balance. We drop the polarity of superior/inferior. We no longer think that white skin is better then black skin or that fit, attractive people have more value than disabled people. There are evident inequalities in the plight of humankind. Yet there are certain universal laws that apply to us all. We are all birthed and we all die. None of us are special and all of us are a gift to the world.

My photographer friend Bruce photographed a wedding and found out the groom was a brain surgeon. Bruce was impressed and told the groom how he respected his profession. The brain surgeon said, "We all do what we do. You do your job, I do mine. We are all needed." Immediately Bruce felt connection and equality with the man rather than separation based on any kind of hierarchy according to profession.

Self-importance…

Self-importance keeps us from being in Divine flow and Presence. We attract attention to ourselves by interrupting, speaking loudly and hogging the limelight. The ego constantly wants to affirm its existence as a separate entity and has many strategies for elevating us above the crowd.

Let's look at the behavior of always being late. Being late means that people have to wait for us, so we are subtly controlling them. The root cause of chronic lateness is that the person does not feel 'enough'. They are looking to validate themselves by having other people wait for them instead of honoring themselves by showing up on time. It's a way of gaining attention from others.

Another common strategy for feeling special is to talk incessantly. People who bore us with their constant chatter suck our energy as they force us to listen. It's a device for drawing attention to them at our cost.

Dale shared with me that the way he did 'special' in his family of origin was to keep quiet and express himself as little as possible. Stoicism was his way. He held his thoughts and feelings in so that others had to second guess him. It was a strategy for drawing energy to him as others had to laboriously question him to draw out his thoughts.

Strategies for feeling important:
Withdrawal—the idea that others are not worth responding to.
Having a special job that the ego latches onto with strong identification.
Humor and being quick-witted.
Acting out the rebel, thinking that rules are for everyone else.
The know-it-all trivia king.
Loud laughter and telling dramatic stories.
Being late.

The spiritual ego...

The spiritual ego surfaces as we move along our path and start to judge others as 'unspiritual'. We think ourselves as righteous, pious and superior. We've 'got it' and others haven't. This is a huge trap. It separates us by creating exclusivity. We must continue to witness the play of the mind here and make sure we are not pumping ourselves up at the expense of others.

Spiritual arrogance can be especially tempting in the case of those who experience energetic phenomena or who have awakening experiences. We think we've 'attained'. Yet phenomena pass. Only Truth is eternal. Instead, we can move towards humility, recognizing that the Divine spark of God is in all of us and we're all playing our roles in unique ways. If we focus on our similarities rather than our differences, we feel closer to people and more open to love.

As we progress on our spiritual path, certain abilities sometimes show up, such as the gift of healing or the gift of intuition. Yogis call these the 'siddhis'. If we choose to make them special it can block our development and we can get stuck there. We need to see our blossoming gifts as a signpost, not a significant event. We honor our gifts as sacred without them being special.

The opposite polarity to the superiority complex is the part of our spiritual ego that plays the card of worthlessness. We take on a mantle of false humility and play small. This negates our light and prevents us from rising to our true potential. It denies faith in our work and ourselves. I can confess to this. I have not always trusted my own ability to model Divine Will. I have had doubt as to the power of the work I do, doubts about my own light. Now I see that is part of my spiritual ego that wants to compare me with my teachers or mentors and judge myself as 'less than'. The truth is, we all have unique qualities and gifts. We each have something valuable to share.

Making others special...

The first people we make special are our parents. In our young eyes they are Gods and can do no wrong. Then we go to school and worship our teachers. We want their approval and attention. In addition, our education system trains us to be competitive and to value winning. We learn value-judgments, comparing ourselves with others. Then we fall in love. Now there is the soul-mate, the only person on the planet who can make our dreams come true! Without them life is 'less than' and we would die with misery. As we get older, we may seek a guru, a teacher who 'knows'. Some of us even give up all our money to teachers in return for a special place in their attention field. Finally we have children. They are special to us and like the lover, we are often blind to their faults

The problem with putting people on a pedestal is that at some point their shadow aspects emerge and they topple off with a resounding thud! Their specialness flip-flops into worthlessness and we suddenly see clearly the true nature of our hero. As mature adults, no one should be an authority over us. If we make anyone special we are giving our power away to them, no matter how enlightened they are. We can appreciate teachers' Presence and wisdom, but let their gifts remind us that we have it all inside too!

Specialness vs. humility...

Humility is a prerequisite for enlightenment. With humility we empty our egos and no longer judge ourselves or others. We stay centered and neutral and use our energy impeccably. In this place of being ordinary, the light fills us. The movie "Forrest Gump" beautifully illustrates this. It depicts a person who is not necessarily smart but has humility, innocence and purity of heart in abundance. He allows life to flow through him without holding onto judgments or expectations. The movie shows how a simple, ordinary man can create an extraordinary life full of Grace.

Karma yoga (selfless service to others) is a great way to experience humility. When we focus on the needs of others our selfish egoic demands dissolve, purifying the heart and dropping us deeper into humility. Another way to create humility is to commit to an entire day of not expressing our opinions! Or for even more of a challenge, take a day of silence. In this quiet place we get to observe ourselves and others more fully without the need to respond verbally. It's quite an enlightening experience to try this—I highly recommend it!

Special events...

There is a difference between making an event special and making it sacred. Making an event special is an invention of the ego that places an expectation around the event. Sacredness contains a feeling of connection, either with others, the Self, or the Divine. The ego drops into the background and there is a sense of universal connectedness. It feeds the soul. There is an underlying sense of reverence and humility, which allows great joy to seep through our being. Any moment can be a sacred moment. It all depends on us and our attitude.

Life has highs and lows. We get married, have children, parents die, we get sick…there are many events that we could deem special and significant. But the truth is, everything passes in time and there is nothing that hasn't happened before and won't happen again. When we let go of making 'big' events special, we are able to move through them with more clarity and with less of a come-down afterwards. If we only live for the weekends, the holidays, or the days spent in the arms of our beloved, we miss out on so much of life. Can we celebrate the flat times too, the ordinary days of our lives? As we activate our witness and observe *what's so*, we can be grateful for each precious moment, appreciating the sacredness of all life.

I was recently contacted by a major TV cable channel who wanted to film one of my yoga retreats for an upcoming TV documentary. I could have been very nervous and made it terribly significant. The truth is, these people are doing a job. It's ordinary for them. They are filming me doing my job. Instead of overreacting I was able to welcome the TV crew into our yoga family and everyone was relaxed about the entire process.

Unique yet ordinary…

Eventually we move into a place of balance where we see ourselves as equal to all. We transform egoic pride into dignity. We see the truth that none of us are special, but just like snowflakes in a snow bank we are all unique, all cells in the body of God.

Examples:

One of my friends was a talented massage therapist. Her clients loved her massages and received great healing from them. My friend thought that she was 'doing' the healing and became very pleased with herself. She thought she was special. Eventually my friend became ill and weak from working too much and had to stop doing massage. Her 'special healing gift' never returned. She understood later that her healing abilities had been a gift from God. She had been caught in the trap of identifying herself with the gift.

My friend Bruce, the wedding photographer, has noticed a curious phenomenon. He tells how the brides who make their wedding day 'super-special' by spending outrageous amounts of money on the event, with the most lavish dresses and the most opulent plans often seem the most stressed when the big day arrives. On the other hand, some families are more easy-going and pull everything together with creativity rather than money, focusing more on enjoying the gathering rather than having everything perfect. These weddings are often more joyful and relaxed, as the pressure of the 'specialness' of the event and the attachment to its perfection is less.

My teacher, Leslie, was in South Africa visiting an orphanage with some friends. They started playing 'ball' with the children. Leslie soon noticed how the westerners all had comments and judgments about how the ball was thrown. "Jolly good shot" they would say, or "Too bad." But the South African kids made no comments. They just laughed and smiled and delighted in the game just as it was. They didn't judge the throws or catches. To them, none of it was special, yet all of it was delightful.

Exercises:
1. Write down all the ways that you make yourself feel special.
2. Examine your prejudices. Write down beliefs you hold about how we are not all equal e.g., races, professions, gender, poor, ugly, old, ignorant, handicapped.
    Then trace back the roots of these beliefs to see where they came from.
3. See whom you have made special in your life. How can you empower them instead?
4. Do a square on 'Desire to be special, desire to be worthless' (see Chapter 7).
5. With a partner: "I think I am special because…." Partner replies, "Is that so?"
6. Discussion: How can we celebrate our magnificence whilst remaining grounded in humility?

"We are all insignificant in the grandeur of the creation—but we are also vital to it as it would not exist in the same way without us." Anon

16.
HOW CAN I CELEBRATE?

Celebrate—you have a precious human birth!

E xistence is made of the stuff called joy and ecstasy is our natural state. It arises out of nowhere because it is everywhere. When we have unburdened ourselves enough of our limiting thoughts and beliefs, this ecstatic state can pop up at any time, leading us to feel that life is a celebration!

Celebration is a state of delight where we experience joy and happiness in everyday life. This inner joy permeates our lives, infecting each moment with a deep appreciation for the Creation and for the opportunity to witness life on the planet. We feel it as a deeper form of gratitude. We don't just say "Thank you." We say "Yippee!"

We share this joy with friends. We come together to play, love and laugh, allowing our energies to flow into each other in ways that enhance us all, raising our collective vibration. Then there is the quieter, inner celebration of life as it presents itself to us, with all its magical opportunities for growth and enjoyment.

Celebrating together...
In these times of change it is more and more essential that we establish conscious community, a group of like-minded souls that encourage us to remain uplifted and aware. Our quality of life is greatly enhanced by developing a community of playmates. We get together to celebrate in whatever format attracts us. We may dance, sing, meditate, chant, hike or just hang out.

If we don't have a big house to invite people to, we can be a little creative. One of my English friends organizes summer picnics in the park where we play Frisbee and softball and have a totally marvelous time. Another friend sets up darts matches at the local pub. There are endless ways to be creative when it comes to having fun!

Having been born British, I come from a culture where any excuse for a party is a good one. People in Britain love to get together, down the pub, out for tea or at friends' houses. Going out with your friends is a matter of extreme importance to the Brits. The laundry can wait. The grass can be cut tomorrow. So what if it's raining! Today let's party! It was a bit of a shock to me when I moved to the U.S. and discovered that Americans didn't celebrate with each other with quite the same enthusiasm. With longer working hours and fewer holidays than Europeans I found many American friends just too tired for much social life. Loneliness is widespread and the craving for community paramount. So I took on the role of event planner extraordinaire. To my delight, people responded to invitations to celebrate with enthusiasm! Our events have become renowned for the joy and togetherness that is shared and for the wonderful spirit of love that permeates the gatherings.

As well as regular satsangs and jnana yoga groups, we invite local musicians to play at my house; we have potluck suppers and movie nights. I don't worry if my house is not perfectly clean and tidy. People see it as the community house and will even pitch in and help me with house-cleaning if necessary! The perfection of 'place' is not important. What matters is having a venue for our tribe to gather.

When we stop taking everything so seriously and lighten up, our lives become much more enjoyable. Happiness allows our energy to flow into others and we open ourselves for our friends' energy to flow into us. This sharing becomes a prayer, a sense of unity and oneness. Sometimes at my house our gatherings end with everyone lying around on big pillows on the floor, a big mush pile of bodies, like little puppies! Our personal boundaries dissolve as we melt into group energy. It feels blissful.

Celebrating each moment...

Celebration does not have to mean extravagant parties. It is just as meaningful to celebrate the ordinary moments of life, finding a passion for all that we do. When we are alone, we can celebrate by being grateful for everything in our life, taking time to connect with the joy in our hearts that's always there. We can smile at the sunlight, laugh at life's intricacies and just be happy. We appreciate Nature, people, music and the arts. All that has been created is for us to witness and enjoy.

If we need some coaching in this, all we need to do is find some young children to play with. Joining in their world of imagination, delight and wonderment, we get to see a fresh new viewpoint where very small things can be a victory and cause for celebration. Can we see this planet not just as an earth school, but also as one great big Disneyland, giving us precious opportunities for entertaining experiences? There are times when I feel overwhelmed with wonder at the magic we have created on the planet; air travel, cell phones and internet, helping us to stay connected with others in faraway places. We truly live in incredible times.

Laughter and happiness…

We probably all know some people who have everything material going for them and are nothing but complaining and miserable. On the other hand, there are others who are in much less fortunate material circumstances and yet who are joyous, always keeping a cheerful demeanor and infecting those around with their love and good cheer. Happiness is a decision we make. It has little to do with external circumstances. We are happy when we love and accept our lives just as they are. We are unhappy when we are resisting our lives, demanding that circumstances be different.

I know a teacher who says that God wants us to be happy. It's our birthright. We can see fun as our God-time and devote ourselves to finding more and more creative ways to enjoy ourselves! We celebrate life by massaging, singing, dancing, jumping for joy, enjoying a leisurely lunch, surprise birthday parties for friends. Playing inspires our relationship with life. We feel nourished and uplifted.

Laughter is one of the most healing and uplifting things we can do for ourselves. We are total when we laugh and the mind cannot think. Try laughing out loud and doing a mathematical problem at the same time! It doesn't work. Laughter, like dancing and singing, raises our vibration and energy. It's an instantaneous way to lighten up. We can even make it into a meditation. Spend five minutes a day laughing uncontrollably and see what a difference it makes. Laughter is Divine! It's a prayer. If we are having a down day and need to raise our spirits, we can jump up and down with our hands in the air shouting "ho!" Or do anything silly that makes us laugh!

From suffering to pleasure..

Gurdjieff, the Russian master, remarked that the western mind is addicted to suffering. He found it a challenge to get his students away from emotional dramas so they could be in a place of joy and easefulness. Along with drama, we are still hooked into the puritanical work ethic, which dictates that working hard is good even if it isn't fun. This is an outmoded idea! Life doesn't have to be a struggle! Work can be a celebration if we perceive it that way and relationships can be joyful opportunities for growth and togetherness.

Some misguided people, especially those trained in formal religions, think that having fun and experiencing pleasure is not spiritual. They attach a value to misery and deprivation and feel guilt about experiencing sensory pleasure. This is another arrogant belief that goes contrary to our very nature. According to ancient tantric texts, cultivation of happiness without attachment or guilt can actually help prepare us for deeper levels of spiritual ecstasy. We keep expanding into higher and higher levels of bliss.

Our senses wish to be delighted. We all enjoy good food, the smell of fresh flowers and hearing beautiful music. We appreciate the beauty in our lives and also see it for what it is, mere passing pleasure. It is unrealistic to expect this sensory pleasure to give us lasting satisfaction, so the practice is to appreciate it all whilst not forming attachments of wanting endlessly more.

Celebrating the shadow...

Celebrating our shadow can be rich with opportunity for expansion. For example, it's possible to be so conscious that when we feel the contraction of a fear we immediately turn it into a tingle of excitement. We celebrate it as something new, beyond our known and our familiar comfort zone. Fear faced with courage brings us great satisfaction and much cause for celebration.

We can choose to expand around the aspects of our lives that we resist, such as our triggers and disappointments. We celebrate our triggers, hunting them down with glee, seeing each one as a new opportunity for healing. We celebrate our disappointments, because each time we are disappointed our mind knows that it did not find the fulfillment we were seeking. One day we finish playing out all our desires and there's nothing left but to look inside, to drop into awareness of Self. There's no more room for hope that input from the external will fulfill us.

We embrace our shadow side as well as our magnificence and say 'yes' instead of 'no' to our challenges. When we dissolve resistance, we experience more energy and are better prepared for the next step of our journey. We are open and available for new possibilities.

Keith is a painter but he wanted to be a spiritual teacher. However, that did not support his family financially. He was feeling frustrated with painting and was struggling to get jobs. He realized he had a nice business that paid well and made homes beautiful, but still the resistance was there. So he decided to fall in love with his painting business! He saw painting as a love affair! As a result of this new relationship with his profession, great new job offers poured in. His frustration dissolved and every workday became a joy.

Celebrating God!...

We sing praises in churches but there are countless more opportunities to raise our spirits by celebrating the Divine. One way is to offer up praise for the food we eat, a simple yet valuable ritual that actually changes the energy of the food! Blessing food is a ritual for our jnana yoga group. We always say a prayer of gratitude for the food and the cooks, and then offer up our prayer to the Divine with a resounding chorus of 'jai ma' which means 'whoopee God!'

Taking moments during our day to feel blessed by Spirit working in our lives is a way we can continually celebrate God. We feel joy for the way it is. Especially if we are depressed or troubled, thanking God for the blessings in our lives can shift our energy and help us feel better. There is always so much to be grateful for!

The question, "Does it honor God?" can be a yardstick for living with respect for the Creation. We add the ingredient of love into everything we do, taking good care of our homes, plants and animals, treating everything as an expression of the Divine. We love our cars, keeping them clean and well-maintained. We 'feng shui' our homes. We honor our neighbors by treating everyone as the Divine in human form.

There is an ashram in India where the entire practice is one of seeing God in everyone. Any stranger who walks through their gates is celebrated as though they were Jesus or the Buddha. The love and sweetness of the monks there is a transforming experience.

Examples:

I'm big on celebrating birthdays. For my fortieth, I asked my friends if they would entertain me, so they put on a cabaret. My women's group became The Pointer Sisters for the night. My other friend, Victoria, the stand-up comic, ribbed me mercilessly, and my composer friend, Mike, created a bongo piece especially for the event. It was tremendous fun and everyone said they had a great time rehearsing their acts and planning the whole event. One hundred people came to the celebration and such was its success, more cabarets have happened since then in our community for other peoples' birthday milestones.

Iwona's teenage daughter Joanna finds it hard to throw anything away and her bedroom is a mess! Iwona wanted her to clean the bedroom and met with some resistance. So she made it a celebration. She put on rock and roll, lit candles and incense and made it fun for Joanna to clean out the room! Together they celebrated getting rid of the clutter!

My friend Doug says that his dog is his best reminder of when to celebrate. The dog loves to swim and so Doug takes him to a nearby lake and together they jump in. Doug says that experience always pulls him out of his doldrums and back into the joy of life.

When Osho, the famous spiritual leader died and was cremated in his native India, thousands of his 'sannyasin' students gathered to celebrate his passing with a festival of dancing, singing and clapping. This was how he wanted his death to be celebrated.

For the last few years I have had the pleasure of taking groups around the world with the prime directive of having as much fun as possible. It's my job and my passion to locate the most beautiful places to visit and design a varied and uplifting program. As well as regular hatha yoga practice, we have gone cave-snorkeling in Mexico, zip-lining in Costa Rica, elephant-riding in Thailand and white-water rafting in Bali. Playing together as a group, eating great meals and yet still returning to yoga practice every day creates a bonding experience equal to none. We are a temporary family of light and love and I have seen people go through great transformations as a result of letting themselves open to this much fun, love and community.

Exercises:
1. Look at your social calendar. Are you happy with it? Are you having enough fun in your life and connecting with your community? If there is room for more, write an action plan as to what you are going to do about connecting with more people.
2. For one day, every time you speak to someone else, imagine that you are talking to the Divine. Notice how this reverence sets the tone for your conversation.
3. Write down why you appreciate yourself, your accomplishments—an ode/tribute to yourself!
4. In small groups: Each person stands up and has two minutes to say why they are wonderful! The group witnesses their magnificence, cheers them on and then claps and celebrates them at the end!

"The master key is to celebrate everything"—Osho

17.
WHAT'S THE CHOICE?

Without awareness there is no choice. We run on automatic, robots of reaction. With awareness, that is, by developing our witness, we can have choice. We are no longer pawns being blown around in the wind. We can be Spielbergs writing our own screenplay of life. If we don't like it, we can choose a different role, a new way of being.

The biggest choice we make is where we put our attention and energy. That is the essence of our free will. Do we focus on personal drama and all the judgments, opinions and concerns that constantly float into our awareness or do we drop our attention back into the true Self, and rest in THAT? Do we choose to stay firmly rooted in the quagmire of the material world or do we jump wholeheartedly onto the path of consciousness as a pillar of light? This chapter explores ways to use our free will to help us realize our maximum potential as a being of love.

Are we choosing to expand or contract?
Every cell and atom in the universe is constantly expanding and contracting. We are too. Our energy is always moving in one direction or the other. Most of the time we are unaware of this movement, we are unconscious. We walk around in a contracted state, wearing armor from past hurts. We are angry, resentful, resistant, blaming and judgmental, all energies that intensify contraction in our energy field and in the physical body.

We literally feel a tightening in the muscles when we contract. The problem is that we get so used to this habitual contraction that it seems normal. Then one day we go and have a massage and the therapist finds knots in our muscles and we become aware of our tight bodies. Or in a hatha yoga class we find a pose that shows us where we are holding tension. These activities are helpful to remind us that we are not yet in a state of full acceptance and openness. There is still contraction in the body to be worked through. Ideally this is not so. Open, aware people have muscles that melt like butter to the touch. There is simply no holding or resistance. What fun to experience life in a body like that! The good news is, we can all be there.

Our bodies give us the biggest clue as to whether we are expanding or contracting our energy. If we think an angry thought we notice the muscles start to clench, the jaw tighten. Sensitive people feel the energy body pulling in closer to the physical body. It's like we are saying 'no' to the universe. This resistance lowers our vibration and fuels our sense of separation, our attachment to personal will. Then if we think a loving thought about someone we adore, or we relax into acceptance of *what's so*, we notice our breath begin to deepen, our muscles soften and our energy field expand again. This is the energy of expansion. We are saying 'yes' to the universe and our vibration increases.

We can notice the energy of contraction and expansion in our everyday lives. Somebody criticizes us and we naturally react with a contraction. We become aware that we have tightened in some way. If we are conscious of this we can make a different choice. We can choose to expand instead. We breathe a little deeper and say an internal 'thank you' for the interaction, knowing that everything is always for us and not against us. We consciously choose to relax our muscles and stay in a place of expansion.

A great tool to help us here is to remember not to take anything seriously! None of today's dramas will be important in ten years' time so why get upset now? Nothing really matters. The universe is neutral. It's only our egos that attach meaning to the events of our lives. We can choose to ignore them!

The week we discussed this in jnana group one of my students got stopped by the police for speeding, a situation that holds huge potential for contraction! My student stayed in her witness, breathed deeply and thanked the policeman for alerting her to her speed. He let her off!

Are we choosing to raise or lower our vibration?

Having the intention to use all actions to raise our vibration is an empowering prime directive for our lives. The higher we vibrate, that is, the higher our frequency, the better we feel, the more we attract what we want in our lives and the quicker we can process our ego/mind illusions.

We are constantly faced with life choices that can help to keep us at a higher vibration. We get up in the morning. What do we do next? Do we stagger to the coffee machine and turn on the TV news or do we drink some pure water and settle into a meditation to start our day? Who do we choose to spend time with? Some people suck our energy and bring us down to their level of negativity. Others uplift us and we feel high in their presence. What do we do for a living? Do we come home exhausted from spending eight hours at a job that drains our precious energy or do we have a career that nourishes us and supports our creativity? What are we eating? Foods all have their own frequency. Generally, live, organic foods have the highest frequency and processed, packaged food the lowest. Drugs and alcohol smash our frequency. Chanting and spiritual practices lift it. Music affects our frequency. Mozart's music has been shown to improve learning and concentration whilst muscle testing studies show that people grow weak when exposed to rap or heavy metal music. Having fun and doing what we love lifts us. When we are happy we are vibrating more strongly than when we are depressed and our life-force is weak.

What thought processes are uplifting? We may have a dead-end job, but if we are grateful for the income opportunity and cheerful with our colleagues we can raise our vibration, despite a tough environment. Yet we could be sitting on a beautiful beach in Hawaii full of mean, hateful thoughts that are lowering our vibration. If our mind is full of resentments and judgments we are creating our own personal hell of suffering. On the other hand if we are thinking loving, grateful thoughts or are dropped into a deep state of Presence where we are not paying attention to the mind, we are in a place of peace. We choose to be happy. Or to suffer.

Are we choosing to stay in awareness or thought?

Most of us spend way too much time in our heads. Our minds are constantly active with their habits of evaluating, worrying, reminiscing, fantasizing and blaming. Yet we only need our minds for activities such as planning, organizing or getting a job done. We become habituated to giving attention to the mind all day long. It is an addiction that keeps us out of Presence and the richness of life.

Allowing our awareness to be fully present to what is going on is a life-changing practice. Each moment is full with vibration, textures, sounds and sensory input. If we tune into these things rather than listening to our mind-chatter, our whole perception of the world changes.

I find when I tune into my sensory perception, my energy field expands and I start to lose the sense of 'I'. It helps me to empty. The thoughts in my head start to subside and I pay less attention to them. It's as though the mind can run, like the TV being on, but no one is watching. Sometimes I can even feel that buzz of existence coursing through my veins. It feels ecstatic, relaxing and wonderful.

One great exercise to help us stay in awareness is to spend a day focusing on the experience of the skin as it goes through our day. What does it feel like to wake up and feel the bedclothes on the skin? To feel the warm water droplets in the shower? To put on body cream; to touch ourselves or be touched; to feel our pet's fur; to touch the computer keys…every moment has potential for a rich, sensual experience if we tune in to it. The habit this helps us to cultivate is one of enjoying what is present and being full with that rather than always wanting more gross stimulation from outside sources. It is a good foundation for happiness.

We can use the constancy of our breath to help drop us into deeper Presence. Taking a 'breath break' to observe the breath helps to deepen the breath and relax us. We can pick a common trigger to remind us to do this. For example, every time we scratch our head or touch our face it can serve as a reminder to watch our breath and feel gratitude for our life.

Are we choosing fear or love?

How often have we thought, "If there is a God, why doesn't he put an end to the atrocities that are happening on the planet?" It can be hard to understand how our society has got into such a mess unless we see clearly the destructive nature of fear. Fear doesn't leave much room for anything else in the psyche. It engulfs us, directing our behaviors towards defense, attack and retaliation.

We've been given a gift of life, of free will. We were given free will so we could create new expressions of divine harmony, love, music, art and poetry. It was never intended that we use free will to create poverty, war or disease. Yet when we choose to be in a state of fear, rather than love, we manifest this ugliness with which we are all so familiar.

The most powerful way to change our world is to examine our own perceptions and see where fear is overriding our natural state of love and trust. Do we believe that everyone is out to get us, steal our possessions, make us wrong or persecute us in some way? This thinking creates a need for us to defend or attack. Or do we see each human as a beloved, a sacred expression of the Divine in human form? Fear cultivates the energy of separation. Love cultivates the energy of unification. Transforming fear into love is a major component of the spiritual journey.

Debby has her own business and was often fearful about lack of money. She felt competitive with others when her business was slow. Once she caught this behavior, she changed it by bringing this fear energy into her heart, blessing her competitors and affirming that there was enough business for everyone. This expansive energy not only helped her feel better but resulted in attracting more cash-flow into her business.

As we progress with our understanding of how the human mind and emotional body function, we see more clearly how our programming has damaged us all. We have fallen into the illusion of separation and subsequent fear, crammed into this limited body/mind. Fears tend to be greatest in those who received only minimal love as children and only love can heal those fears. With this understanding we have the choice of keeping our hearts open in all situations, no longer sinking automatically to the level of fear and anger. In the face of conflict we can bring the energy of fear up into the heart, where it is transformed into love. Forgiveness, tolerance and acceptance help us to stay in this state of love no matter what happens around us.

True compassion is loving those that seem unlovable, the murderers and rapists. We see the lack of love in their world and the depth of their wounding that caused the behaviors. Rather than condemning or judging, we pray for love to be sent to them so they can heal.

Sandy's brother was in prison. He was afraid and angry. He wrote Sandy a vindictive, threatening letter. She did not react with fear when she read it, but felt great compassion for her brother's pain. She decided to send the letter back to her brother. She did not shame or berate him; she just refused the 'gift' of the letter. So her brother got to keep his gift. He said later that it changed his outlook on life when he got this letter back. He re-read his own mean words and his heart melted. His sister's love enabled him to transform.

Are we choosing to wake up to Truth or stay in the illusion?

Practicing jnana yoga and choosing to examine ourselves creates a big shift in our vibration. When we are willing to take responsibility for our lives rather than remaining unconscious and ignorant we can start to unravel all beliefs and patterns that no longer serve us. We drop the illusion of victimhood and start to see that on a deep level we have chosen every event in our lives in perfect harmony for our own development. However we cannot plumb the depths of our shadow without having a lot of light at our disposal. We must have a strong connection to God and our higher self. We can do this through anything that fills us with light, such as prayer, meditation, yoga practices, constantly being in witness, and accepting ourselves fully with the utmost compassion.

'Waking up' is the process of seeing through our illusion of separation and fear and discovering the Truth of who we are. Our choice to do this is the highest use of our free will. We can choose how fast or how slow we want to go in our process of waking up, communicating with our angels and guides to help us. We ask guidance to remind us when we are off-track and are about to make an egoic choice. For example, the ego says, 'be busy', but the soul wants stillness to be creative. Our choice to pay attention to our soul energy, our Essence, rather than the voice of ego brings a magical quality to life.

All these choices are facets of the same theme. Being in our heart, in a place of love, present to the moment, raises our vibration and expands us. We use our free will to stay conscious about these choices moment by moment.

Examples:

A romantic relationship had ended and with that distraction gone I decided to commit 100% to waking up. I disciplined myself to thirty minutes minimum daily meditation and one hour of either hatha yoga or walking in nature. I decided to clean my bodily temple by going on a liver cleanse. I ended up flat on my back for two weeks with diarrhea and cramps, hardly eating or going out. My addictions and desires fell away. I no longer craved chocolate, wine or relationship. During that time a friend of mine died which led me to confront my own death. I discovered I was fine with dying too. In fact it got me to appreciate each moment with a new freshness. I lay around in my hammock hardly thinking, just being. Yet I wasn't suffering. I saw this as part of my sacred process. It wasn't fun or comfortable but it was OK. And I trusted I would pop out the other end having been dissolved and reconstituted, ready for my next level of service. I did.

Michelle was afraid of being hurt again in relationship. She armored herself against intimacy and refused to let anyone in. But deep down she wanted love and a partner in life. She noticed she was jealous seeing happy couples together. Once she realized she was responsible for this energy of fear and defense, she shifted her attitude, blessing any couples that she saw, affirming that she too could have that again. She chose love over fear and eventually the universe responded and she attracted a new loving relationship into her life.

One day I tripped in my garage and sprained my ankle. I had never been injured before! It hurt a lot and I could not walk on the foot for days. I had to use crutches. However I did not resist the experience. It seemed new and challenging for me. I embraced it, expanded around it completely and found many gifts in the slowing down I was forced to do. My friends came to be with me and help out. I received their love. I felt a greater sense of Presence. As I integrated these lessons, my ankle healed very fast and I was walking normally within a week!

Exercises:

1. Write or discuss how you are currently creating separation in your

world with fearful thoughts. How can these be transformed with love?

2. Make a list of your daily activities and put them under two columns: vibration raising and vibration lowering. See where you can commit to making a change.

3. With a partner: Discuss what is stopping you from a 100% commitment to waking up. Where are you still holding illusions that block you from aligning with Truth?

4. Make room for Presence. Adopt a Zen-style approach to daily life and slow down enough to be relaxed and aware at all times. Place 'post-it' notes around the house to remind yourself to 'breathe, feel, be, or slow down'.

LETTING GO OF THE PERSONAL 'I'

Surrendering our identification with the personal 'I' yields the fruit of jnana yoga practice. We drop our stories of the past and who we think we are. We give ourselves up to the Divine.

As we empty ourselves of desires, fears and attachments, the answer to the question, "Who am I?" can reveal itself. The ego is experienced as dissolved and there is no more sense of separation as we merge our awareness back into unity consciousness.

18.
WHAT'S THE STORY?

"Keeping our past alive is like investing our life force into a mausoleum"—
Carolyn Myss

I am sick and tired of hearing the same old stories pop out of my mouth! Like a record stuck in its groove, I hear myself repeat stories about the past, what happened to me when I was young, how I was wronged and stories of what other people think about me which I assume to be true. I have become bored with my story. I've noticed that when I am telling my story or thinking it, I am no longer here in this moment. I am off in my mind somewhere else, which takes me away from Presence.

Stories reinforce belief systems that keep us in suffering. These belief systems are thoughts that define our identity and shape our attitude towards life. Like a carpet we rolled out behind us, we keep rolling out the same carpet in front of us again and again, creating patterns of recurring experiences.

There is always a choice: story or Presence. It's up to us to decide where we focus our attention. With the story there is stress and suffering. Without the story there is innocence and peace. Dropping our story means letting go of beliefs, grudges, blame, resentments, and interpretations of reality. This allows the mind to return to its quiet state of empty awareness. It is a pre-requisite for waking up to the truth of who we are.

Why we have stories...

Our conditioning, our cultural and personal history, has helped us to create our story. It is shaped by what other people want us to believe about ourselves and what we see around us and accept as normal. If someone in authority tells us we are dumb, lazy, or weak we believe that. If society tells us that fulfillment comes from having a big house, a successful marriage and children, we believe we are entitled to that. None of this is true. If we live in our maximum potential we disconnect from these ideas and open up to all things being possible in any moment.

Our mind files and stores the stories we have created very neatly. We can regurgitate with effortlessness our 'poor me' stories about how terrible our childhood/ marriage/ business/ illness was, what our lovers did to us and how the world has treated us, not to mention statements about 'who we are'. I am a person who is never late, loves cats, always cries at movies. I am THIS, I am not THAT. We label ourselves with our absolutes and stay stuck in these labels, limiting our potential. These labels and stories create self-fulfilling prophecies. Over time, we become what we think about most as our story about ourselves gets continually reinforced.

Marcus tells a story about himself that he is fat and unattractive and that attractive women will not want to date him. He manifested what he told himself and stayed single for many years. After coming to jnana group he decided to drop that story and choose a new attitude. He even got a haircut and bought some smart new clothes to feel better about himself and to reaffirm his new story that he was, in fact, attractive. As soon as he did this he noticed women flirting with him. Eventually he started a relationship again.

Our stories get their life force from our resistance to letting them go. We hold onto them because they feel comfortable. We are addicted to our personal drama and are used to bonding with others in this way. For example, if we have a broken heart, we think we are suffering. We have a story about why it happened, who did it to us and how. We may be very invested in this story, in our role as the victim or in being 'right'. Our ego feels self-righteous and important by playing the blame game and involving others in a personal drama that draws attention and energy.

Everything that happens in the universe is just an event. It is neutral. It is only the meaning we attach to the event that creates a charge for us and furnishes fuel for a story! In other words, our perceptions and beliefs create our dramas. We tell stories, be they conscious or unconscious, that substantiate our belief systems. Our stories prevent us from truly experiencing what is going on in the moment and from connecting fully with other people. In order to experience life directly we must drop into a state of beingness and let go of all thoughts and interpretations, otherwise we will continue to have disconnected and unfulfilling experiences.

"Some people don't just have a story; they have a library!" Whitney Campbell.

Unplug from the past…
The past is gone. In this moment there is no story. We are just here. And

in this moment we get to choose again, fresh and new, without the shackles of our past. We can step out of our own prison. Our Presence is the key that unlocks our shackles. We don't have to forget what happened to us, but we can stop analyzing it or using it as an excuse about how it affects us now.

Sam had always told himself he was a lousy businessman. He had gone bankrupt years ago and lost one of his businesses. Now his new business was going through a rough period and Sam was worried about repeating his past failures. He became aware of this negative self-talk but decided to let go of his 'lousy businessman' story. He started to make different choices and above all held himself in a new light of being successful. Sam's business is doing great now!

When we invest energy into our past we have less for now. It robs us of power and slows our ability to co-create. We wait longer for healing guidance because we are depending on our known rather than on Creative guidance in the moment. Our ability to act spontaneously is reduced.

Becoming anonymous...

Being around our family of origin or old friends who hold an image of us in a certain way locks us in the past and reinforces old patterns and stories. Often family and friends are invested in keeping us where we were as it helps them to feel more comfortable about themselves. If we don't change then they don't have to either.

When we travel to foreign cultures, nobody knows us. If we don't speak the local language, our communication is limited to essentials and is devoid of unnecessary chatter. We are anonymous and can drop our story more easily. There is no one around to perpetuate our past and our limiting beliefs except ourselves! What is a story without someone to tell it to? When I'm anonymous I have noticed I feel free, more available and open to new experiences. This experiment in becoming anonymous requires a willingness to be alone for a period of time. In my experience it is a highly revealing time for introspection and witnessing. I strongly recommend solo travel or vision quest for this purpose.

How to drop our stories....

Once I became aware of the garbage about myself that I would repeat like a squawky parrot, my stories started to ring hollow in my ears. They sounded boring, false and inauthentic. It took a while to drop them completely, but each narration left me feeling more embarrassed at my limiting self-talk. Now I can witness a story wanting to spew forth from my mouth and nip it in the bud before it leaps out by relaxing into the present moment instead.

We can also use inquiry to relieve our suffering by questioning our grievance stories. We take a statement of our opinions or beliefs, such as 'He should not have taken my money' and ask if we are sure that this is a true statement. The answer here must always be 'no', as we can never really know for sure that our opinion is true. Then we investigate to see if this thought creates stress in the body or mind. Generally it does, and if so, we can see clearly that our thoughts are disturbing our peace.

This inquiry is a great tool for bringing us back into Presence and revealing the effects of our confused thinking. It offers us clarity and understanding, a doorway into clear perception.

Our stories keep us looping through images and thoughts from the past and take us out of the present. They are necessary only if we are using them to illustrate a point from our life-experience. Otherwise we can let them go. The only place we really have power is in each moment. When we let go of the story there is nothing for the ego to hang onto. Any pain can be experienced simply as pain and the suffering will not be there in the same way. Pain is inevitable but suffering is optional.

If there is pain, we just experience directly who is feeling the emotion. We don't resist the emotion but dive into it, to discover the nature of the wound, where it is, and who is wounded. When we directly experience emotions with full awareness we discover they are not really there! In the light of our own Presence, emotions dissolve and peace is revealed. It is our true nature, a changeless state underlying all other temporary states. For example, if we feel sad but leave behind the story of sadness and experience the sadness directly, we will find that underneath the sadness is peace. It's hard to find sadness without a story attached to it.

Other peoples' stories...

We all have friends who love to dump their sad stories on us. Misery loves company. We can stop this by choosing not to give the drama queens and kings our energy. When we stop supporting that role, they will stop playing it—at least with us. Even in a marriage, our partner's story belongs to them and we must resist the tendency to buy into their negativity.

It is important to determine where our friend is at and at which level we can best serve them. We must find out if they are on a spiritual path and available for conscious feedback or if they just want to tell their sad story. We can ask the person if they just want us to listen, if they want advice, or if there is something we can do for them. Story-tellers normally want validation, but this drags both parties into a downward spiral of negativity.

If our friend just wants a listening ear, one good technique is to simply repeat their story back to them. Mirroring does not signify agreement; it is just a reflection that helps our friend to feel heard, and gives him or her the opportunity to hear their story from another source. It is an act of Presence and love.

If our friend is available for conscious feedback, we support and hear their process without indulging their story. This means we stay in our observer state, not hooking into the drama or fueling their fire. Where appropriate, we encourage them to use their life events to witness their unconscious behavior, shining light on limiting beliefs and patterns. We give their story minimal energy, yet keep our hearts fully open to our friend for their awakening. In this way we uphold a vision of this person's highest potential.

In the end...
The more we identify with our witness and the less with our ego/mind, the less our need to tell our story. Instead we leave the past in the past and focus our attention on the present and what is alive and real for us now. Any need for storytelling dissolves into the richness of the moment.

Examples:
Edmond won a school poetry competition at the age of five and his prize was to recite a poem in front of all the parents at a concert. He spent three months practicing for the big day. When it finally came, he felt frozen with fear and could not remember the poem. Feeling ashamed and angry at himself, he left the stage in tears. This incident set up a belief that he was not good enough and couldn't ever get it right. Unconsciously he has been telling himself that story ever since. His life has been a litany of failures, in business and relationships. But now that he is aware of this story and pattern, his old behavior can change. He has unhooked from the belief. There is no more block to attracting success.

My friend Laura went away for the weekend to write music. She took a hotel room and settled in to write. She told herself she needed peace and quiet to be creative. The next day there was a parade going on right under her hotel window; a string quartet was playing and trumpets were sounding down the road! She watched herself

149

get annoyed—then decided maybe she was telling herself a story about her need for peace and settled down to write anyway, despite the noise.

John had cancer and the doctors gave him six months to live. He decided not to believe their story about his health. Instead he embarked on a quest to heal himself using alternative methods. He is still thriving many years later.

Joan was going through a turbulent time in her relationship. She would talk to her friends about her partner and get nothing back but negative comments about him. So she decided to stop telling her relationship story to everyone for a month. It helped her keep clear about what she really wanted without advice from her friends. She noticed she saved a lot of energy for herself and was able to act from the clarity she had gained.

Exercises:
1. Stop telling your story to yourself and others! Every time you see yourself about to do it, just stop in your tracks. Or prefix your statement by saying, "In the past...."
2. What did someone tell you that you believed about yourself? E.g., you are worthless, messy, stupid.
3. Notice why you uphold other peoples' stories. Do you want approval, attention, love, empowerment, belonging, to be needed, connection? Is this the best way to get it?
4. Choose your favorite grievance story. Write it down. Review it, then take some of the key statements of belief and inquire into them. Are these statements true? Do they disturb your peace? If so, what do you gain from holding onto them?
5. With a partner, discuss: What you are holding onto from the past that prevents you from feeling whole right now?

"While we tell our stories of unworthiness and unhappiness there is within us already an ocean of happiness! Let it reveal itself!" Gangaji

19.
HOW MAY I SURRENDER?

Prayer of surrender:
"Dear God—put me where you want me to be,
With whom you want me to be
Doing what you want me to do."

What do we think of when we hear the word 'surrender'? For me it conjures up a 'laying down of arms'. In a way that's exactly what it is. A letting go of the struggle, the struggle that pits our will against the Divine and the struggle to uphold the illusion that there really is an 'I' (the ego-personality). There are two levels of surrender to consider. One is at the level of the personality where we start to align our personal will with Divine will and let go of our attachments, our resistance and our need to control. The deeper level is the surrender of the separate 'I', where we give ourselves entirely to the Divine.

Surrender requires a 100% acceptance of *what's so*. Not 99% or even 99.5%, but total, absolute acceptance in each moment, with no resistance! Full acceptance frees us from our identification with the mind and its opinions. We are freed to reconnect with our Essence and deep peace is the result. The past and the future no longer have power over us and we can be fully present in the Now. We surrender the hope of a better tomorrow and relax into this moment, just as it is. We let go of our demands that things be the way we want them. We realize it is a hopeless request. That's why so many prisoners wake up to their Divine nature in prison. Their situation is hopeless and all that is left to do is to surrender to it. Imprisonment can be their greatest gift if their surrender is absolute.

Letting go of the struggle...
Life can be like a tug-of-war. We pull on the rope, resisting, struggling and fearing what will happen if we stop. This constant battle eats our peace and agitates us into states of tension and stress. Yet if we would only put the rope

down and relax into accepting our lives just as they show up, our hell could change to heaven in an instant.

The rope we tug on represents the illusions of our mind, opposing reality; mental pictures in our head that drive us crazy and take us out of our inherent blissful nature. We want life to be the way we think it should be. We project unrealistic expectations onto ourselves and onto the world. When things don't go our way, we tug harder on the rope, blaming, resisting and making up stories about how we were wronged. Like the rope under tension, our minds become rigid and taut.

We have been given certain unique qualities and tendencies—our intrinsic nature. Some of us are equipped to run marathons; others are better suited to be parents or artists. Some of us are happy sitting alone in caves as the contemplative mystic; others possess a social nature that drives them to create community. We are genetically, culturally and personally predisposed in certain ways and struggling against those predispositions creates misery and frustration.

I am not by nature a mystic, still I have yearned for mystical experiences to show up. Why is it that my friends get the visions, the colored lights, the heavenly voices and the burning bushes but I don't? I have wanted God to show himself dramatically. Yet that is not how He has manifested to me. For me, 'dropping the rope' has meant letting go of the desire for it to be that way. I have relaxed into being grateful for the gifts I do have and have accepted that my relationship with God is perfect just the way it is.

I observe many spiritual seekers struggling to emulate a blueprint of the way they perceive a spiritual person should live. However, the blueprint is outdated. It may have worked to awaken Eastern students in the last century, who lived in ashrams with gurus as their teachers, but we live in different times. New techniques are available for the Western mind-set and ordinary people from all walks of life are waking up without having ever done any traditional spiritual practices.

As a younger seeker of Truth, I was drawn to the yogic path. I became vegetarian, practiced celibacy for a while and did four hours of chanting and meditation a day. I ended up anemic, frustrated and bored. These 'traditional' prerequisites of awakening were not useful for me, personally at that time. I still did not know who I was.

Struggle creates ego. I used to think, "I am pure, I am a yogi." Yet if anything, my personal 'I' was strengthened through a sense of glorious martyrdom about my practice. I felt superior and self-righteous, dedicated to my spiritual struggle to 'get somewhere' and 'obtain enlightenment'. Struggle is the opposite of flow. With flow, we accept whatever state we find ourselves in. We are relaxed. There is no suffering. We can flow or fight, accept or resist. That is our choice.

We can experiment with this if we have a headache. Instead of resisting the pain of the headache, we can just allow the pain to be there, let it flow through. Then we get to see that even with pain, happiness can be present.

Surrender vs. apathy and resignation...

Surrender is not apathy. It is not repression or denial. We don't just roll over and play dead, accepting everything blindly. Struggle has its place. A mugger tries to steal our purse and we struggle to retrieve it. Maybe we have cancer. We accept we have the disease and still look for ways to heal ourselves. We accept ourselves fully in the moment and know at the same time there is always something we can do to expand into a higher potential. However, there is a difference between pushing ourselves to be different and moving gracefully towards expansion.

Surrender reconnects us with our natural Divine state and joy flows into our activities. It leaves us wide open to Divine Inspiration, where energy flows through us and we can work tirelessly and fearlessly for the good of all. Martin Luther King Jr. wanted to change America's policy of segregation. God worked through him to invite the changes that resulted in greater equality for all races. For this greater good he sacrificed family time, personal desire and eventually his young life, the ultimate act of surrender.

When we don't surrender...

When we persist in using our willpower to act out our ego's desires and make things happen, certain things start to occur. First we get exhausted. It takes a lot of our energy to resist and struggle. Then, if we insist on hanging on tenaciously, life beats us up. We get sick, miserable or suffer calamities. These disturbances force us to look closely at what we are doing and make a change. If we don't, the change comes in an even harder way, like the blow of the sledgehammer!

When I was married I followed my husband's career path and became a Realtor with him so we could work together. Neither my passion nor my skills were suited to that job. I was clearly going against God's Will for me. Despite initial success, our real estate empire eventually collapsed like a house of cards and I lost everything. As a result of my resistance to Divine Will, the universe kicked me violently away from activity that was not my highest calling.

We must be willing to face reality and clearly see where we are in denial and fear. How often do we stay in jobs or relationships which have run their course far longer than is healthy, rather than admitting the energy for them has left? Better to let go of dead-end situations and move forward into new experiences than to resist change.

Saying 'yes' to *what's so* is an important component in our surrender; 'yes' to exactly what is real and true right now, even if this entails acceptance of a painful situation. It's our resistance to life as it truly is that fosters denial and causes us discomfort and misery. As we all know, resistance causes persistence! The degree to which we let go of this resistance is the degree to which we evolve and have peace.

Not my will but Thine...

Our lives are fueled by our desires. Desires themselves are neutral. They are just desires. It's our ego's attachment to them that creates imbalance. If the desires are stimulating hope for a better tomorrow, they create resistance to the present and prevent us from loving our life just as it is. We must be willing to experience anything and cling to nothing by continually dropping back into our witnessing position and saying 'yes' to all that arises.

If we are too attached to our wishes, we leave no room for the Divine to bring us what would really give us joy. It's fine to give the universe an 'intent' for a desire to become manifest. But then we must let go and surrender our effort and control. We must relinquish using our will to manipulate outcome and instead let God show us whether it's in our highest good for this outcome to manifest. We trust whatever happens as a manifestation of Grace. If I find myself unclear as to God's will for me I say, "Look God, I'm feeling stuck in a fog of confusion and I need help to see clearly, so please make my next step completely obvious!" Then I watch and wait for a pointer or sign to guide me in the direction I need to go.

Viktor had divorced, lost his company and ended up lonely and penniless over Christmas. He was furious at God and dared God to strike him down! After a five minute temper tantrum of fully expressing his anger, he dropped to his knees crying and uttered the words, "I give up. Show me what to do with my life." A sense of calm overcame him as he surrendered to the situation. As he dropped deeper into that, he heard a voice telling him to play his keyboard. He started to play the most beautiful music. Melodies flowed through him, as though his fingers were being guided by unseen forces.

His willingness to change opened up a new career as a concert pianist. He is now a successful recording artist with a dozen piano CDs to his name.

If we are driven by the phenomena of pleasure then we will constantly be grasping for bigger, more and different pleasures. This constant desire to fill ourselves from the external is what creates our internal hell of the hole that cannot be filled. The cycle is never-ending until we stop and lay it down. It is not that we renounce pleasure; what we release is our unreal expectation of what sensory pleasure will bring us. We let go of our grasping attitude. Now we are ripe for a true surrender and the possibility of a lasting, fulfilling happiness. We have chased our dreams and found only temporary satisfaction. Yet our very disillusionment contains the key for a new way of being.

When we are surrendered we live life as a response, controlling neither events, activities nor our desires, but instead being available for what wants to happen. We don't hold on to anything. We adopt a 'letting go' state of mind, emptying ourselves of our concerns, fears and ideas, our attachments and our attitudes. We allow the flow of the universe to guide us without resistance. Our control has kept us safe and brought us to where we are. But now it is time to jettison the engine of that particular rocket ship and drop deeper into the true Self.

Letting go of the 'I'...

My teacher Gangaji once told me I needed to 'die before I die'. "But how do I do that?" I wailed back at her, at which point she hit me on the head with a plastic baseball bat to encourage me to drop out of my ego and go to a deeper level of Presence where such a question would just not arise. Many years later, I experienced dissolution of the self that felt like a death. Julia was gone. There was no one there to have opinions and judgments, just a witness to observe life going on. Finally I knew what Gangaji had meant.

In order to surrender to the Truth of who we are we need to let go of our sense of identity, every concept about ourselves, the world and others. We must surrender thoughts, attachments, emotions, hopes and dreams, our conditioning, doubt, suffering, labels, the past, ideas about the future, our point of view—all the elements that define us as individuals. Finally we die to the old way of being, yet what dies is only our illusion of what we think we know. What remains is our true eternal unchanging Presence.

Courage...

Surrendering our identity takes courage, courage to leave behind all we have known and how we define ourselves. It requires a ruthless cutting away of the past, a willingness to stay in the unknown, to experience the heart of annihilation. We become vulnerable and open, like little children. This can be scary. Fear of losing control and losing our individuality arises. That is why, for our surrender to be complete, we need to have already transformed most of our fears and negative emotions. We must know ourselves inside out in order to lose ourselves.

When we are willing to give up identifying with 'me, my life, my attainments', that is, when we are ready to stop serving the personal 'I', then we can serve God. We can ask the unseen realms for help in our surrender. We give up any concepts about what this help will look like or when it will come and just relax in the faith that if we are really ready and willing it will come. We can use every circumstance of our lives as an invitation to deepen the surrender; good times, boring times, pleasure, discomfort. In every moment we can let go more and more deeply into Presence and acceptance.

Remember Abraham? God asked him to kill his favorite son. He was willing to do it. Then, at the last moment God stopped him from performing the act. Surrender requires this kind of willingness. We must be willing to make a fool of ourselves for God, to take risks, even if it makes us vulnerable. After all, even Jesus was nailed to a cross.

How do we know when we have surrendered?

On the personality level we know we have surrendered when our internal struggle stops! When we struggle with an emotion or feeling such as despair or frustration, we give it life and energy. Our imagination keeps it going. But when we are really accepting and present there is no more struggle. We just drop into what is happening in each moment with gratitude for all of it. The deeper this surrender, the greater our capacity to be present.

On a deeper level, we know we have surrendered when egoic desires and fears have fallen away and we have offered ourselves fully as a conduit of God's love. In clearing the grasp of our own ego we have released our resistance to love, so nothing more stands between us and our Divinity. There is no more struggle, no more control, just appropriate action in the moment in a relaxed, calm manner.

Our minds may fear surrender as a disempowerment, yet surrender is not a defeat. As we let go of pretending, hiding and indulging we drop into greater and deeper levels of Presence. It may sound like we are giving something up but actually the opposite is true. In our surrender the Grace that is always present can manifest itself and illuminate us. We feel we have finally come home to our Source.

Just let God have you. Surrender to being found. Turn yourself in!

Examples:

Surrender is about being available for Divine Will in the moment. My friend Bruce wanted to come for our jnana group one night but just before he left home, he got a call from his daughter-in-law who needed his help with a car problem. So he went to help her instead with no mental struggle. He just surrendered to the moment and accepted that this was what was needed.

When I was growing up in England I had a best friend named Sally. Our parents were also best friends and she was like a sister to me. We were normal English girls, full of hopes and dreams for a wonderful future. Neither of us showed any signs of any spiritual leanings. Years later Sally had a transformative experience through prayer when she felt the oneness of all of us and experienced the Holy Spirit entering her being. She laid down her personal 'I' immediately and devoted herself to helping others from that moment on. Her calling took her to India, Pakistan, Indonesia and Thailand, where she lives today. She has raised four children yet works tirelessly with AIDS orphans and the handicapped, who are considered 'cursed' in Thai culture. When I visited her in Thailand I was amazed and inspired by her joy and the light that shines through her so evidently. She shines this light on everyone she meets and it was incredible to watch people open up and respond to her in the space of a few minutes. My dear friend Sally is a shining example of a surrendered soul who has given up material desires in favor of working as a servant of God.

Mother Teresa's surrender was so absolute that she completely let go of her fear of death in order to perform her work with the dying of Calcutta. Although constantly exposed to diseases and the extreme suffering of the miserable, forgotten street people of India, she nursed them and ministered to them in their final days with no thought other than loving her brother as herself. She rarely got sick and lived well into old age.

Exercises:
1. Pick a situation you have been resisting. Practice accepting it deeply, loving it.
2. What is your sacred cow, the one thing you think you couldn't live without (e.g., sex, family, work)? What would you be willing to give up for your God-realization? Practice offering this one thing to God as a prayer.
3. Write or talk about one thing you have desired and ways you have struggled for it. What have you learned from the struggle? Why do you think you want this?

Then, give it up; surrender it to God saying, "If you want me to have it, I am available for it. If not, I trust it's not what I need right now." Let go of the struggle of trying to get it!

"Anything you accept fully will take you into peace. That is the miracle of surrender." Eckhardt Tolle, 'Power of Now' tapes.

20.
WHO AM I?

In the beginning, as our soul began its journey into the third dimension, we made a contract to forget that we are Source in order to be total in this experience called life. A band of forgetfulness was placed around us so that when we incarnated we would perceive ourselves as separate, individual beings, free to create as we wished. This device did its job well. Our souls have had many adventures as individuals and the Creation has been expanded and furthered. But things are changing. The time for that is over. Now we are being asked to remember who we really are. Any time we wish to disconnect from this experience of duality we can go home, meaning that we identify ourselves as Source instead of this mind/body vehicle. It's like in the movie, "The Matrix," when Neo is offered the choice of taking the blue pill, which would have kept him in the illusion, or the red pill, which would disconnect him from that reality and open him up to the Truth. If you are reading this, you have taken the red pill.

The fundamental error of life is our identification with the body and the mind. This mind/body vehicle we inhabit is programmed. We are not. It's like we are driving a certain type of car in this lifetime. We are not the car, it's just a vehicle. We are the one who knows we have a body, mind and emotions. The body does not know it is a body.

Self-Realization means fully grasping that we are not our egoic programming. We don't need to feel bound by the programmed structures that we took on in childhood. When we disconnect from everything we think we are, we will find a limitless awareness. As the mystics say, "Thou art That."

Starting to disconnect...

We have no true allegiance to our persona. The more we strengthen our ability to witness, the more we experience detachment, where our inner thoughts and feelings are something we notice as though they belong to someone else. When we disconnect from past and future, and disconnect from our emotions and thoughts, something else occurs within our being. A blissful state, that 'peace that passeth all understanding'. We don't try to stop the mind—that doesn't really work for many people—we just observe it and disconnect from it. Then we discover the place in us that is empty yet full. A state of 'isness', beingness, the pure, neutral witness, our God-self.

Most people live their whole lives completely unaware of this state. They live identified with ego and mind, their personal 'I', which has opinions, demands, desires, fears. Yet it is possible to step out of this false-identification. We cultivate non-attachment and strengthen our witnessing skills. Then, as we stop taking our life-dramas so seriously and let go of our self-importance, we become available for this natural state of awareness to creep up on us. Grace meets us half way.

Starting from the place of our normal, conscious reality we may not encounter this state right away. We might feel better, the box of our awareness can expand, but we still experience ourselves as separate. But in the seeking life starts to work; our vibration increases. We feel better, life is more delightful. We feel more peace and joy, and little by little we may slip into these unnamable states. We become more present, our thoughts trouble us less. We accept more. The more we can be in the moment with the least mind chatter, the more everything can unfold for our highest potential. We can expand into greater realizations. It is a never-ending process of expansion.

Identification...

When we identify with something, there's a subject and an object, and we create duality. Me and that. The 'me' has defined an outside object and becomes protective and possessive. 'Me' perceives life in the separate lane. We identify ourselves as a personality, but what is that but a series of habits and gestures? It's as though we are saying our dress had a wonderful day yesterday.

We wake each day and once again don the garments of our identity. We slip on our name, our occupation and our stories about who we think we are. But who were we before we compared ourselves to others who have names and stories, before we evaluated ourselves? We believe we are our name, body, history, emotions, thoughts. Yet if we look inside ourselves for the 'me', we can't find one. The personal 'I' is seen to be non-existent. It is experienced as real in that there is an awareness of the body and mind, yet it is realized to be unreal, like a play or movie. We notice that feelings and states come and go and constantly change and recognize that this is what the ancient seers of India called 'maya'—the illusion of the world playing through us.

The world would have us believe our purpose is to enhance the power, prestige and comfort of the body/mind vehicle. Yet striving to fulfill worldly goals keeps us stuck in our illusion of separation. Then...surprise! We are not who we thought we were. When we break the identification with ego, body, senses and thoughts we can merge back into pure consciousness. What we thought of as 'our' consciousness turns out to be only a part of a consciousness caught in the illusion of separateness.

Journey into neutrality...

Neutrality is the doorway to a higher level of vibration and consciousness which makes it easier for us to experience the Self. Neutrality is the balance that takes place in our energy field when we are neither attracted nor repulsed by anything, that is, we have no latent desires or fears. As we let go of more and more of our conditioning and our automated responses to life, neutrality can start to show up. This deepens and eventually we see we are attributeless and therefore we are everything too. All of it and nothing.

Much of our study in this book up till now has helped to bring us to a place of more neutrality. The squares processing technique discussed in Chapter 7 is particularly useful for this. We can take any feeling we are having, find its opposite and process it into neutrality in the form of a square. The more we practice staying in the state of witness, the more this state of neutral mind can show up. It is the gateway to an experience of our eternal Self. Our witness watches what arises, what passes through. Mind has misery, or torment, body is uncomfortable. We watch it all from that disconnected state without giving it energy. We acknowledge what is happening without attaching too much importance to it.

Neutrality is a detached state but is still full of juice and movement. It is certainly not boring! We still experience all the states, but without identifying with any of them, even the states of ecstasy and bliss.

Stepping out of the box into true freedom...

This is the journey of the spiritual warrior. It is scary because we are headed into the unknown. We are familiar with our conditioning, our personality. It fits like an old glove. It feels safe. Yet at some point along our spiritual path we reach a stage when we can take a break from exploring thoughts, emotions, feelings, sensations and circumstances and are ready to explore the Self. THAT. The Presence of Being that is who we are.

Much of our jnana yoga work is aimed at bringing our unhealed mind into balance. We could call this 'healing our neurosis'. Asking, "Who am I?" gets us focused on our Divinity rather than our neurosis. An awakened being (guru) always sees our Divinity and if we are sensitive we feel that mirrored back to us. This feels good, it uplifts us. That is why sitting in the presence of awakened beings encourages our own awakening more easily and is highly recommended. They are the candle that lights the unlit flame inside us.

There is an 'I' who is free. We can call it our I AM Presence. This Presence is permanent. Experiences are just overlaid on the Presence. Presence is not an experience. It is bigger than the mind and the emotions and is always there regardless of state. Meeting this I AM Presence is freedom.

"I AM THAT" is the most profound statement we can make, an affirmation of the highest order that starts to dissolve the human condition/ego. By affirming it we can become it, so it's helpful to keep it in consciousness, to keep dropping into it. We can make it our mantra!

Meditation...

Sitting quietly, undisturbed by the outside world is a wonderful practice and helps us to access our I AM Presence. In the stillness, all we are not can drop away and we can plug in more strongly to the energies of Divinity. This recharges our batteries, relaxes us on many levels and allows us to empty our minds of worthless chatter so that we are available for the light from Source to pour into our cells.

There are many books and tapes on meditation techniques. Personally I find it easier to drop into Presence whilst listening to a guided mediation. I use Leslie Temple-Thurston's "Burning Karma" or "Gateway to Samadhi" (order through www.corelight.org). My active mind is easily distracted and listening to a tape disciplines me to sit for at least half an hour whilst I relax to the soothing words being spoken. Some people can sit just fine in silence and others like to play music. It really doesn't matter how we do it. But I find that it is important to spend some time each day disconnecting from external stimuli and going within to remember once more my true nature and to keep my lines of communication with Source open.

Neti neti...

The great Indian Saint Ramana Maharishi encouraged his students to ask the question, "Who am I?" The response would always be in the negative. "I am not this body, I am not this thought, not this emotion." The Sanskrit terminology for this is *'neti neti'*, which means 'not this, not that'. My jnana students have found this to be a great tool for disconnecting from their life-dramas and alleviating their suffering. It helps us remember we are bigger than whatever is troubling us. 'I am not this broken leg/agitated mind/broken heart'. *Neti neti* is a great practice for helping us to witness every state that passes through us from a place of dis-identification. However there is another level here too.

The great mystic Osho told his students that "Who am I?" is not really a question because it has no answer. It is a device, not a question. We can use it like a mantra. The mind will supply many answers yet we must reject them all. As long as it remains a verbal question a verbal answer from the head will be supplied. Eventually we can drop the verbal question. It can remain just a vague idea. When we are not asking it in language and just the feeling of the question is settling inside our center, then there is no need of any answer. It is not the business of the mind. The mind will not hear that which is nonverbal, and the mind will not answer that which is nonverbal. Instead we will get the feel, the taste, the perfume. Then at some point, a miracle happens—the question disappears. The question has no more props to support it, so it just collapses. We drop into the Presence that we are.

In this way the question is a device that cuts the very roots of the mind so only the silence of no-mind is left. In that silence there is no question, no answer, no knower, but only knowing and direct experience. The deeper we go, the more we are filled with the feeling of limitless being, immortality, blissfulness. This feeling has a truth about it. Then we can know. When the knower is no more, the knowing is.

The ultimate goal of yoga...
Asking "Who am I?" together with the stripping away of who we are not, leads us to a place beyond the mind where nothing remains to describe the individual being but the true, essential nature of the Self. There is no more sense of separation, just awareness and unity. Life becomes a flowing, timeless meditation. The ego is experienced as dissolved and the individual perceived as a cell in the body of God, a unique expression of the oneness of all that is. The word 'yoga' in Sanskrit means union and it is this union with oneness that is yoga's ultimate purpose.

Examples:
I spent some days alone on a desert island in Thailand where there were no mirrors! I was alone and was mostly silent. Not being concerned with appearance and not voicing my usual opinions and attitudes allowed me to sink much deeper into a sense of my own I AM Presence. My sense of 'I' started to disappear. As I emptied out, there was more fullness, more bliss. There was no Julia left to feel lonely.

My teacher Leslie has been a mystic from an early age. She is now at the point where there are just no thoughts in her mind, unless her mind is needed to respond to a question or solve a problem. Her awareness rests constantly in the blissful state of emptiness, no longer identified with ego.

When I visited Osho's ashram in India I spent many days in silent, anonymous meditation. After a while I noticed that I no longer cared where I sat at dinner, what I ate or who sat with me. These preferences evaporated. I felt like a transparent ghost floating around. There was no more 'I' to care about these matters. Presence was dominant rather than the personality. And in that empty place a blissfulness arose within me that was beyond words. It felt incredibly freeing and illustrated the value of losing the 'story of me'.

Exercises:
1. Spend some time every day dropping into awareness and Presence through meditation.
2. Make "I AM THAT" your mantra.
3. With a partner: ask each other the question, "Who are you?" Reply in the negative, e.g. "I am not this body, not this thought."
4. With a partner: Ask each other the repeating question for about three minutes each, "Who is experiencing this moment?" Switch over three or four times. Notice that although there is really no answer to this question, our failure evokes the sweet perfume of deeper Presence.

Meditation to let go of the 'story of me'...

S it comfortably, close your eyes and take a deep breath in and out. Start to let go. You've taken the red pill. Now it's time to reprogram your biocomputer and discover the truth of who you are. All old files will be downloaded onto a CD and put aside.

First, download your name, family history and the story of your past. Put the disc safely away—it can always be picked up later.

Next download your body image, bodily sensations, feelings, and aches and pains; stories about health. Then download all memories, belief systems and ideas. Put the CD away. Now download the personality, the character and all egoic desires, preferences, judgments and fears. Put the CD away.

Now all stories about love, spirituality and enlightenment. Put it away.

Now download the thinking process. Put it away too.

And notice what is left.

Are you still there? If so, what is looking out from behind your closed eyes now? Don't look in the CDs for answers; just find the direct truth of what's real.

Drop deeper into that, the Presence that you are. Can you tell where this awareness ends?

What is its limit? What happens if you try to lose this awareness? It's this awareness that was there before we were born and is always with us. Can you feel the body sitting in the awareness?

Is there any separation between your awareness and that of someone else, or is it all the same stuff?

Can you begin to see that the story of you, the personality, ideas and history have all been overlaid on top of this awareness, yet that awareness is always there, our true Self, waiting for us to drop back into it and drink of its essence.

Taste it. Is anything missing? Does it feel whole? Rest in THAT.

Now slowly open the eyes and come back into the room. See if you feel like putting the CDs back in or leaving them where they are!

GUIDELINES FOR GROUP FACILITATION

Gathering together regularly in a group is the most powerful way I have found to work with the information in this book. As a group, we support each other in our process of unraveling old behaviors and can quicken each other's healing. For example, someone else's issues may trigger something for us to look at that we otherwise would not have considered. We realize that we are not alone in the issues that confront us and can feel comforted to have this community of friends who are supporting us on our path of self-awareness. This is vitally important, as feeling alone in the world is one of the biggest challenges that many of us face. To be surrounded regularly by a group of non-judgmental, like-minded, supportive people is a gift indeed.

Establishing Procedures

In my jnana yoga groups we always begin by setting the spiritual mood for the session. It is this context of spirituality that sets a jnana yoga group apart from a plain therapy group. I like to bring everyone into a circle sitting on the floor. If that doesn't work for some people then use chairs, but be close together, knees touching if possible and holding hands to establish a feeling of intimacy right from the start. As facilitator I bring the group together with a short centering meditation and a prayer. Here is what I say. Please feel free to use the same verbiage or modify as you see fit.

"Let's all come together in a comfortable sitting position and close the eyes. Allow the tail-bone to drop down into the ground and lean back into your sit-bones. Relax the shoulders, lift the chest slightly to straighten the spine and allow your attention to go to your breath, gaining a sense and an awareness of breath consciousness. On the next exhalation just allow the events of your day to slip softly from your shoulders, melting into the ground and letting go. Let go of all that has gone before and all that is yet to come and be here now, affirming that this is a time for healing and nurturing and for mending the bond of trust with your God-Self. Take a deep inhalation and lengthen the spine and inhale once more and join in oms."

I lead the group in three 'om' chants. We follow with a prayer that goes something like this:

"Great Spirit, we ask that you bless this gathering tonight and give us the courage to open our hearts and speak our truth. We ask that you imbue our discussion with wisdom and compassion and guide us gently on our path of Self-discovery. We offer up our prayers and invite all your blessings down upon us. Jai Ma (this means 'Whoopee God'!)

In new groups I start out by welcoming them all to jnana yoga and introducing myself. I then go round the circle and ask the students to introduce themselves to the group and say why they are here and what it is they are looking for. That way we begin to get a sense of each other and everyone feels they have already participated, so shyness starts to dissolve.

Next I discuss the guidelines for group participation. First and most important I get everyone to agree to a condition of confidentiality in order to make the space safe and sacred for our sharing, which is often of a very personal and intimate nature. We agree that everything that is discussed does not leave the room.

Next we talk about commitment to attendance. I like to run my groups in four, six or eight week sessions. I allow new students to join us during the first two weeks of a new session but after that we close the group and no new people can join in. I do this to create more intimacy within the group. When the group is closed and the people get to know each other better, a deeper level of communication and support can occur. So if the student decides to join we ask them to commit to showing up each week. If they have a business meeting out of town or are sick and cannot attend, then they commit to calling or emailing me so I can tell the group why they are absent and also give them the next week's homework. That way they still feel part of our process even if not physically present.

Then I talk to the group about how we share. I ask them to focus on talking from personal experiences rather than from the mind's perspective of ideas and thoughts. I encourage them to make 'I' statements to help them do this. I also warn them that for the sake of time and in consideration of the group, that I will act as hatchet girl and if anyone is having difficulty keeping to personal experiences when they talk, I will gently interrupt them and try to bring them down out of their heads and into their hearts. I also encourage them to be brief and to the point so that everyone in group who wants to share has time to talk.

I tell them that I am not the guru. I do not have all the answers—although I do have some jolly good questions for them! We are here to share our wisdom as a group and if they have a perspective or experience that is helpful for someone else then they should please raise their hand and speak. However when one person is talking we all listen attentively and do not give commentary until that person is finished. To let us know that they are done talking the person sharing may just say, "I'm complete," else I will ask them, to be sure before anyone else chimes in or before I share my perspective with them. Some groups like to use a 'talking stick' of some kind. It could be any object at all. The person talking holds the object and puts it down when he or she is finished. This procedure allows the speaker to feel heard and honored. It creates a feeling of respect amongst group members and is particularly important when sharing sensitive issues.

Content

I find it works best to have a theme for each session. This book is conveniently divided up into segments which lend themselves well for this. If a group is brand new, I suggest starting with the first four chapters to get the basics covered and go over terminology, such as the concept of witness consciousness and what we mean by asking, "*What's so?*" Whichever set is chosen, the students are given the homework of one of the questions to keep in their consciousness for the week. We talk about the question and how the student might use it to raise awareness. It's always helpful to add a little from our own personal experience, too. Make sure everyone has understood what is being discussed. The new awareness the students have during the week will then be used as the focus point for the next meeting. Ideally, students will actually read the relevant chapter in the book to give them some more background on the question and to see how it pertains to their lives.

The first week of running a new group is tricky because the group has not yet been given any homework. This is a good time to go over the principle aims of jnana yoga and introduce students to its history (see "20 Questions for Enlightened Living", my previous book, for history of jnana yoga.) I then like to ask each person in turn to talk a little about where they are currently challenged in their lives. This helps people to get to know each other and begins to open the arena for discussion. Then we talk about the theme chosen for the series and go on to discuss the homework.

Facilitator Challenges

Over the years I have run into a few challenges in facilitating group dynamics. For example, there are some people who love to give advice. The word 'should' often pops up in their speech. When I hear this happening, I jump in and ask the person to speak from personal experience, rather than repeating things read in books or that others may have said. Sometimes the person is unable to do that and just remains quiet. I often find that habitual advice-givers will not stay in the group, as their cup is possibly a little too full for them to really learn.

Some people love to ramble on and on in great technicolored detail about every facet of their story. Not only is this boring for other group members, but it's also a good indication that the person is talking from a place of mind rather than an experience of the heart. One trick here is to give people a time limit. I sometimes use an egg-timer! When their time to speak has run out I invite them to get to the point quickly or we will move on to someone else! This often helps them to dive into the heart of the matter where they can share their deepest truth and be vulnerable, so real transformation can then take place.

Some people tend to dominate groups that allow free-for-all sharing; other people often remain quiet. A technique here is to go around the circle from time to time and ask everyone to give their perspective on a certain issue or question. That way even the shyest people are encouraged to speak and can be heard and supported by the group, and the more talkative people get to practice active listening!

The Close

Just before we close our group I ask group members if there is anyone they know in need of healing or support. Students will speak the names of friends and relatives. We imagine them in the center of our circle and send them our healing energy as a group. If a student who is present is not feeling well we invite her or him to lie down in the center of the circle so we can focus our healing energy on them too. This type of prayer is very powerful and we have often heard reports of its positive effects.

Next, I invite us all to hold hands and close our eyes. Then I say something like this: *"Just begin to let everything settle down. Relax into your sit-bones and allow the attention once again to be drawn to the breath. Take a moment to absorb all the love and support that's available for you here in this group. Drink it in. Feel fully how it is to be here right now, as part of this circle. Take a deep inhalation and lengthen the spine and inhale once more and we'll join in 'oms'. (We all chant 'om' three times). I'd like to thank all of you for being here tonight and sharing your yoga, your wisdom and your energy. I remind you that true gains come in a personal practice, so play with the homework, value the yoga and above all honor yourselves. And may the rest of your week be filled with joy, love, light and delight. Namaste."* (We all make the gesture of namaste, with the hands in prayer position in front of the chest.)

Building Community

One of the great opportunities of forming a jnana yoga group is that of building up a conscious community. To foster this, we have a potluck supper before group and tea and desserts afterwards, so students have some time to socialize and get to know each other outside the formal group process. This is a great way to establish friendships and continue to enjoy the group energy. What often ends up happening is that students get together on a regular basis outside of our weekly jnana meetings and continue to build on the friendship and intimacy they have found in the group.

GLOSSARY OF TERMS

Sanskrit words and their meanings:

Advaita Vedanta—the philosophy of non-duality, the doctrine that nothing exists except Spirit

Darshan—a gathering to share spiritual love and receive divine blessings, normally in the presence of a guru

Jnana—knowledge or wisdom

Jnani—practitioner of jnana yoga; an enlightened one who knows the Self

Jnana yoga—the practice of inquiring into the nature of ourselves with the intention of seeing the Truth of our being

Maya—the illusory world

Neti neti—not this, not that, meaning not identifying with the illusion of life

Satsang—same as darshan

Shushumna- the core of light that runs up the center of our body

Sutras- threads or verses

Vedanta—the name of different schools of philosophy founded on the teachings of the Upanishads. Concerned with Self-inquiry.

Viveka—discrimination between true and false

Yoga—union

English Words and their Meanings

Cellular memory: emotional memories stored in the cells of our bodies

Cords: energetic ties

Core: our center, the heart of who we are

Duality: divided in two, a term used for describing our world, reflecting its nature of opposites.

Ego: the separate self, the false identity, the conditioned personality which perceives itself as separate from the whole

Enlightenment: an all-encompassing perception of non-separation

Essence: our Spirit, our energy

Grace: a force of divine love, healing and support, which flows to us, especially when we pray for it

Grounded: conscious in the body

Guides: our spirit guides on the 'other side' who are always with us, guiding us through this life

Hole: a tear in our energy field due to emotional trauma

Light: energy from the Divine

Neutrality: a place of balance beyond the swings of polarity

Neutral observer (Witness): the part of us that is able to perceive without judgment the conditioned personality being acted out

Polarity: the opposition formed by negatively and positively charged attributes

Presence: our awareness, full consciousness

Process: using methods of self-inquiry to clear the ego/personality of illusion

self, the: the small self, the ego/personality

Self, the: the authentic, eternal immortal beingness that we all are

Self-inquiry: the practice of looking at consciousness

Self-realization: permanently actualizing direct knowledge of the Self

Shadow: the unconscious side of the ego

Source: God, the Divine

Spirit: the invisible realms

Square: a processing technique for balancing our polarized minds

Story: what we make up about what is so

Trigger: something that causes us to feel a charge of unhealed emotional energy

Waking up/awakening: dropping the illusion that we are this body/mind vehicle and realizing the true nature of the Self

What's so: how it is right now in this moment

Witness: our neutral observer, our awareness

SUGGESTED READING, INCLUDING MY COMMENTS...

<u>The Classics</u>

The Song of God (Bhagavad Gita), **The Chiltern Yoga Trust, South Africa, 1984.** The Bhagavad Gita is the Bible of the Hindus. This timeless classic can be read in three hours—yet it takes a lifetime to absorb its deeper meanings. I recommend finding a class with a qualified teacher to guide you in understanding. There are many different commentaries published on the verses. I find *The Song of God* particularly clear and easy to follow. The commentary is written by Swami Venkatesha, a student from the lineage of Swami Sivananda.

Prabhavananda, S. *Shankara's Crest Jewel of Discrimination.* **Translated by Christopher Isherwood. Vedanta Press, 1970.** The 7th century Hindu mystic Shankara speaks clearly about the nature of the Self and the difference between maya and Brahman. Easier to understand than the Upanishads or the Gita, it is a good introductory book into classic vedantic philosophy, written by a great saint who experienced Truth.

Vivekananda, S. *Jnana-Yoga.* **New York: Ramakrishna-Vivekananda Center, 1955.** Taken from Swami Vivekanandas's lecture tour of Europe in the late 19th century, the languaging and thought processes are dated and hard to follow. However if you can get over that, there are many gems of truth hidden within these pages.

The Upanishads Vol 1—4. **Translated by Swami Nikhilananda. Ramakrishna Vivekananda Center, 1994.** Poetic and profound, these ancient texts are hard to understand yet should be read at least once by all serious jnana yogis, if only to absorb the energies of enlightenment that are still transferred from page to reader.

Gospel of Sri Ramakrishna: Abridged edition. **Translated by Swami Nikhilananda. Ramakrishna Vivekananda Center, 1988.** A diary of a devotee's experiences around this great master in the late 1800s. Comprehensive and full of spiritual truths, yet a little heavy going to read at times.

Osborne, A. *Ramana Maharshi and the Path of Self-Knowledge*. York Beach, Maine: Samuel Weiser, Inc., 1970. A description of the life and times of Ramana Maharshi, the great modern day saint. Excerpts from dialogues with Ramana are included. Fascinating!

Swami Satchidananda, *The Yoga Sutras of Patanjali*. Integral Yoga Distribution, 1990. The classic treatise on raja yoga translated from the 2300 year old Indian text. Much studied by yoga schools to this day. Many of the observances and recommendations proposed by Patanjali cross over into the realm of jnana yoga.

I am That, Talks with Sri Nisargadatta Maharaj. Translated by Maurice Frydman. Durham: Acorn Press, 1982. Transcripts of over 100 talks that Sri Maharaj gave to devotees during the first part of the 20th century. I suggest reading this more for the energy behind the words than for any techniques to be gleaned. This book will drive your mind crazy! And that's the point….

Contemporary Mystics

Anonymous. *A Course in Miracles*. Tiburon, CA: Foundation for Inner Peace, 1975. This is a channeled book that is essentially a course in jnana yoga. Much favored by study groups, the material here is powerful and rich. However, many people including myself find the style long-winded and laborious. It lost my interest before I could get through all of the 1,000 plus pages…

Sri Aurobindo, *The Synthesis of Yoga*. Pondicherry: Sri Aurobindo Ashram, 1971. A comprehensive 860-plus page volume on the value of yoga in our daily world. Not for the meek, this is an intellectual book with many references to the Upanishads and the Gita. Heavy going.

Temple-Thurston, L. *The Marriage of Spirit*. Santa Fe: Corelight Publications, 2000. Highly, highly recommended!!! Leslie is a fully-realized modern-day jnana yogini who offers straightforward and down-to-earth ways of processing our hidden blocks and learning to identify more fully with our witness. I particularly recommend the squares processing technique, which I've outlined here in Chapter 7.

Gangaji. *You are That*. Novato: Gangaji Foundation, 1996. Transcripts of satsang interviews with Gangaji. The simplicity of her message is profound and enters straight through the heart. She invites us to be still, to stop, and let Presence be. Catch her satsangs if she comes to your town—or at least get one on video.

Krishnamurti, J. *The First and Last Freedom.* San Francisco: Harper, 1954. A wealth of wisdom, this book takes the form of questions presented to this modern mystic and his responses. Don't be put off by the awkward style—the richness of the wisdom is worth the effort!

Lowe, P. *In Each Moment.* Vancouver, BC: Looking Glass Press, 1998. A clear, easy-to-follow guide to becoming more awake from one of the most gifted spiritual teachers of our modern day. Highly recommended.

Osho. *The Tantra Experience.* India: Rebel Publishing House, 1978. I love this book! Easy to read, written in contemporary, clear language by Osho, the Indian mystic known as the Great Communicator. This book is intensely about freedom. It opens my heart and liberates my soul. Can't recommend it highly enough!

Poonja H.W. L. *Wake up and Roar.* Edited by Eli Jaxon-Bear, Novato: Gangaji Foundation, 1992. Taken from satsang questions to "Papaji", this book provides the reader with wonderful ways to answer the question, "Who am I?'

Tolle, E. *The Power of Now.* Canada: Namaste Publishing, 1997. Mr. Tolle offers portals to our awakening. Lovely book with many great exercises and points of awareness.

Yogananda, P. *Autobiography of a Yogi.* Los Angeles: Self-Realization Fellowship, 1946. Incredible story of the life of a modern mystic in 20th century India. It takes the reader to meet mythical beings such as Babaji in the heart of the Himalayas as well as chronicling Yogananda's relationship with his guru and personal spiritual adventure. Easy to read and heart-warming. This book helped to wake me up. Highly recommended.

Related helpful reading

Campbell, S. *Getting Real.* Novato: New World Library, 2001. A wonderful, practical guide to becoming more authentic! Complete with guided exercises to practice in every-day life, this is a great book for becoming more conscious about ourselves and how we show up in our world.

Christensen, A. *Yoga of the Heart.* New York: Day break Books, 1998. A sweet book that takes the teachings of Patanjali's sutras and applies them to our everyday world.

Dass, Ram. *Be Here Now.* New York: Random House, 1971. The

book that opened up so many people when it came out in the early 70's...a classic for our times...highly recommended.

IsanaMada. *A Call to Greatness*. San Francisco: Dhyana Press, 1994. A very good guide to becoming more conscious and fulfilling our true potential as humans. Great exercises and information.

Matthews, A. *Being Happy*. Singapore: Media Masters, 1998. I liked this book. Fun to read with lots of cool cartoons, this little book is also packed with wisdom. It's light yet deep.

Ruiz, Don M. *The Four Agreements*. Amber-Allen Publishers, 1997. Shamanic teacher Don Miguel Ruiz exposes self-limiting beliefs and presents a simple and effective code of personal conduct learned from his Toltec ancestors. Easy to read and a good adjunct to jnana yoga.

Tindall, J. *20 Questions for Enlightened Living: Peace and Freedom through Jnana Yoga*. Mt Shasta, 2003. This book offers the jnana yoga student a beginning place of study. The witness is introduced and '*what's so*' is discussed in detail. Subjects explored include forgiveness, love, melodrama, judgment and desire. This book together with the one you are reading creates a complete body of work. If you like this one you will enjoy the other one too!

Williamson, M. *A Return to Love*. New York: Harper Collins, 1992. A modern classic, this book opened my heart. Based on "The Course in Miracles", Marianne brings those teachings to life in an easy-to-understand format. I read this book whilst stuck in a rural Chinese airport in a rainstorm. Yet the Truth contained in these pages pulled me into a state of bliss!

ABOUT THE AUTHOR

Julia Tindall is an instructor of hatha, jnana and tantra yogas and leads workshops and retreats at beautiful places around the world. She created the world's first jnana yoga teacher training program and on-line jnana yoga course.

Julia offers 'satsang', where students sit in pure awareness of the Truth of who they are without identification to the ego.

Julia is the producer of many acclaimed yoga videos including a unique floor-series DVD and the world's first Partner Yoga video. She has a companion CD of meditations that complement the processes outlined in this book.

If you would like more information on Julia's retreats, workshops or videos, please contact her at 916-486-4620 or email juliatin@aol.com.

Website:www.JuliaTindall.com

SEMINARS, RETREATS AND YOGA VACATIONS WITH JULIA TINDALL

Transformational Seminars based on *Your Presence is Enough*

Intensive seminars designed to empower the student in the practice of Self-inquiry. Learn how to drop into Presence by letting go of all that is not Real. Discover hidden patterns from the unconscious that are blocking your true potential; release old belief systems that no longer serve and experience the love that arises when all else dissolves. These unique and powerful intensives will help you gain insight, clarity, and a fresh approach to life. One weekend can change your world forever! Practical, hands-on processes will be used, based on the 20 Questions.

Weekend Retreats

Julia leads weekend retreats in the USA at healing sanctuaries such as Esalen Institute, Harbin Hot Springs, Sierra Hot Springs, and Mount Shasta. The weekends are yoga intensives where the student can immerse in the various yogic practices of hatha, jnana, bhakti yogas and meditation.

With the support of Julia and the group, a loving energy is created that holds a safe and sacred space for transformation.

"I am still so high from the weekend! This is the best group of people I have ever attended a workshop with!"—Andy Andersen, Corcoran, CA

"I woke up on Monday morning after the Harbin weekend feeling as if the world had made the sweetest, purest love to me and I am eternally grateful!"—Lynn-Marie Murphy, Palo Alto, CA

Yoga Vacations

Julia regularly leads yoga vacations to Mexico, Bali, Costa Rica and Hawaii. The trips are characterized by a sense of openness, camaraderie, and free-flow in the spirit of 'lila yoga', the yoga of play.

"I can't begin to thank you for such a wonderful trip. I have never felt so alive and well. The yoga was life-altering and for the first time I felt so much bliss, love and peace.

I will take your love, your lessons of yoga, and think often of my new family I met in Bali!" —Marie Exline, Burlingame, CA

Call 916-486-4620 or e-mail juliatin@aol.com for upcoming yoga retreats or vacations, or visit www.juliatindall.com

VIDEOTAPES, DVDS, CDS AND BOOKS
by Julia Tindall

Safe and sensible learning tapes

BEGINNERS YOGA DVD $28 plus $3 shipping and handling
3 unique beginner sequences in 1 DVD!
1. FLOOR SERIES—This soft and gentle practice helps students get grounded in the basics of yoga. The focus is on breathing into each asana with conscious awareness. The series is practiced entirely on the floor to allow the student to surrender deeply and let go of tension. Suitable for everyone. 1 hour, 15 minutes.
2. SHOULDER OPENER SET—30 minute set of easy-to-follow shoulder movements. Can be done on a chair.
3. COBRA/FROG SERIES—gentle back bends and twists on the belly. 30 minutes.

HATHA YOGA ANIMAL SERIES VIDEO- $25 plus $3 s and h
For the beginner to intermediate student. This one hour video begins with a breath practice and moves on with the animal series of asanas for spinal flexibility and hip opening, leaving the student feeling refreshed and revitalized for the day.

PARTNER YOGA VIDEO—$25 plus $3 s and h
Enjoy yoga with a friend! This light-hearted and fun video guides you through a variety of poses where your partner helps you to open your body, gently and joyfully!

"Thanks for the yoga video—you did a GREAT job on it! Even I can follow it! I love your reminders to continue deep abdominal breathing, keep the spine straight...and relax!" Donna, Fortuna, CA

HEALING MEDITATIONS CD—$15 plus $2 s and h
8 different healing meditations based on the methods outlined in this book. Subjects are:

Forgiveness, saboteur, humiliation, death, story of me, fear, patterns, triggers.

CONNECTING AT THE HEART CD—$15 plus $2 s and h

The perfect CD for creating more love and intimacy with your partner! Julia leads couples through four separate exercises designed to nurture and connect.

20 QUESTIONS FOR ENLIGHTENED LIVING, Peace and Freedom through Jnana Yoga—$18 plus $2 s and h.

Julia's first book takes the teachings of classical jnana yoga and applies them to modern, everyday life in a clear, easy-to-understand format. Discover the monster of attachment that eats our peace; learn to move through lessons more quickly; get acquainted with the workings of the witness. Subjects covered include judgment, forgiveness, love, control and truth—plus many more!

For all inquiries call 916-486-4620 or e-mail juliatin@aol.com

To order any of the tapes or CDs, please mail a check to:
Julia Tindall
PO Box 601872
Sacramento CA 95860
USA

5185172R00110

Made in the USA
San Bernardino, CA
27 October 2013